the diabetes
WEIGHT LOSS DIET

the diabetes
WEIGHT LOSS DIET

antony worrall thompson
azmina govindji • jane suthering

photography by steve baxter

KYLE CATHIE LTD

In association with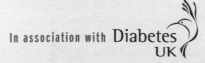

This book is dedicated to the two million people with diabetes and to those who could also be at risk.

IMPORTANT NOTE

The information and advice contained in this book are intended as a general guide to dieting and healthy eating and are not specific to individuals or their particular circumstances. This book is not intended to replace treatment by a qualified practitioner. Neither the authors nor the publishers can be held responsible for claims arising from the inappropriate use of any dietary regime. Do not attempt self-diagnosis or self-treatment for serious or long-term conditions without consulting a medical professional or qualified practitioner. It is vital that you talk to your diabetes care team about losing weight before you start and have regular reviews of your progress.

First published in Great Britain in 2007 by
KYLE CATHIE LIMITED
122 Arlington Road, London NW1 7HP
general.enquiries@kyle-cathie.com
www.kylecathie.com

10 9 8 7 6 5 4 3 2

978 1 85626 644 4

EDITORIAL DIRECTOR Muna Reyal
DESIGNER Jenny Semple
PHOTOGRAPHER Steve Baxter
HOME ECONOMIST Jane Suthering assisted by Anna Helm
STYLING Rachel Jukes
COPYEDITOR Marion Moisy
RECIPE ANALYSIS Dr Wendy Doyle
PRODUCTION Sha Huxtable and Alice Holloway

A Cataloguing In Publication record for this title is available from the British Library.

Colour reproduction by Sang Choy
Printed and bound in Slovenia by MKT PRINT d.d.

For information and support on managing diabetes contact the Diabetes UK Careline: 0845 120 2960 Mon-Fri 9am–5pm *(lo-call rate and operates a translation service)*
Textphone *(for people with hearing impairment)* 020 7424 1031
www.diabetes.org.uk

The following websites also offer helpful advice:
www.leicestershirediabetes.org.uk
www.bdaweightwise.com
www.nationalobesityforum.org.uk
www.menshealthforum.org.uk
www.giplan.com
www.thinkwelltobewell.com

ACKNOWLEDGEMENTS

There are too many people to thank but certain individuals deserve a special mention: My wonderful wife, Jacinta and our two children, Toby and Billie, who suffered from my lack of quality time yet supported me throughout, as well as moving house and office during this period! To Louise Townsend, my energetic and ultra-efficient PA, who fielded hundreds of phone calls from the publishers and who was regularly on hand to smooth troubled waters when the pressures of deadlines took their toll. To my agents, Fiona Lindsay and Linda Shanks at Limelight Management, who keep me from being idle. To my teams at Notting Grill, Barnes Grill, Kew Grill, The Lamb, and The Greyhound, and in particular, David Wilby, my Operations Director, who kept the boat(s) afloat. To Azmina Govindji, who yet again has done excellent nutritional work, and to Jane Suthering. To Jenny Semple, the designer and Steve Baxter the photographer, who have made this book look so good. And finally to Muna Reyal, my editor, an iron hand in a velvet glove and her great team at Kyle Cathie. **(AWT)**

So many people are involved when a new book gets published – it isn't just about the authors. I would like to express my gratitude to my dear friend and colleague Dr Wendy Doyle who has tirelessly helped with the recipe analysis and menu plans. I was assisted with research for this book by Rajni Jambu, student dietitian working with Aparna Srivastava RD, Senior Lecturer in Dietetics at Coventry University. Thank you also to Sue Baic RD from Bristol University, Jacqui Troughton, Advanced Diabetes Practitioner, and the Nutrition and Dietetic Services of Leicester Royal Infirmary. Mountains of appreciation go to my co-authors – we make a cracking team! And huge thanks to our colleagues at Diabetes UK, especially Natasha Marsland, Jemma Edwards and Zoë Harrison from the Healthcare and Policy Team, and to Muna Reyal of Kyle Cathie Publishers, for being so patient and for your guidance throughout this project. **(AG)**

Team work is everything on a project such as this. In the kitchen I have been ably assisted by Anna Helm. Wendy Doyle and I have spent many hours balancing the recipes to fit the necessary dietary criteria and the editorial help from all at Kyle Cathie is unsurpassed. I thank you all. **(JS)**

contents

A word from Antony

There's dieting and there's your diet, two words with very different meanings. Dieting means losing weight whereas diet is the food you eat on a day-to-day basis. What I've tried to do with this book is combine the two so that you can eat well and lose weight at the same time.

A few years ago, I was told that I was at an increased risk of diabetes. Of course I worried that my food life was over so I did some research and realised people with diabetes can still eat well as long as they follow some basic rules. I initially wrote **Healthy Eating for Diabetes** followed by my **GI Diet** and **GL Diet**, which were aimed at people who wanted to eat healthily, especially those with diabetes. Many of us are keen to lose weight and this book, while following the good food principles of my previous books, will also help you to achieve this.

I've managed to lose about 13kg and I want to lose another 7kg, but I'm not into instant 'bikini' diets – they are not sustainable in the long term, are no good for your health and you usually put back on all the weight you lose. I've also been really chuffed with the results of my last three books. So many readers have told me that they have lost weight and some have even managed to reduce or come off their diabetes medication. These are results we should all be proud of and I'm sure this book will have a similar effect.

This diabetes weight loss diet isn't a quick fix. It's a diet that is healthy and will improve your well being as well as your weight and equally importantly I reckon you're going to enjoy it, which will be a bonus. Follow the menu plans, mix and match recipes if you want, but always remember to keep an eye on the calories. The food is so enjoyable you may be tempted to ask for second helpings, so be disciplined, learn to enjoy smaller portions – your body will soon get used to it. Temptation is one of life's biggest enemies so when you go shopping for food write lists and wear blinkers!

My final message to you is to eat well, lose weight, stay healthy and enjoy yourself.

Foreword by Diabetes UK

Being a healthy weight is important for everybody but especially
for people with diabetes. If you have diabetes, following a healthy
balanced diet and keeping your weight in check can help you achieve
good diabetes control and protect yourself against the long-term
complications of the condition. If you don't have diabetes, managing
your weight and leading a healthy lifestyle can actually delay or
prevent the onset of Type 2 diabetes.

In this book you will find handy tips on how to start altering your diet
to achieve and maintain a healthy weight. It is full of delicious recipes
and shows you how to be healthy without compromising on taste.

The following recipes are not only for people with diabetes, but
for everyone who enjoys good food and wants to stick to a healthy
weight.

We hope you enjoy trying them out.

Douglas Smallwood
Chief Executive
Diabetes UK

This section will explain how diet can affect your diabetes and how losing weight can help you to manage it as well as bring you other health benefits.

about the
diabetes
weight loss diet

Introduction

Congratulations for picking up this book! You have taken the very first step in making a difference to your health and your day-to-day life. Being overweight can seriously affect your health, but there are also many other reasons to lose weight. Making realistic long-term changes to your lifestyle can bring huge rewards – whether you want to fit into last year's summer clothes, play in the park with your children or run for the bus, losing weight (and keeping it off) is worth the effort. As you flick through these pages, you will find tempting recipes and practical tips to help you do this – but remember that you should check with your healthcare professional before going on a diet.

This book is intended for people with diabetes who need to lose weight. However, it is also a great resource for anyone who wishes to eat more healthily or reduce the risk of Type 2 diabetes. By trying out these tasty recipes, which have all been created specifically with health, blood glucose control, blood pressure and heart health in mind, you will be better equipped to reduce your risks of developing Type 2 diabetes, especially if you're overweight. Since eating for diabetes is simply a healthy diet, the whole family can enjoy this delicious dining experience. Take a look at the tips in the following pages to help support you with your new healthy lifestyle goals.

If you have Type 1 diabetes, your condition will be managed with insulin as well as a healthy diet and physical activity. At least 30 per cent of people with Type 2 diabetes are on insulin too. Since the recipes and menus (see pages 38–41) are intended for people who want to lose weight, if you are not overweight you will need to allow yourself larger portions. There are also recipes that are intended for weight maintenance, indicated at the top of each recipe by a green marker.

DIABETES – WHY TREAT IT?

Over two million people in the UK have diabetes. Another 750,000 have it but are completely unaware of it. Often diabetes can be picked up when you go to the GP for a routine checkup and it is important to speak to your GP if you have any of the symptoms listed below.

CLASSIC SYMPTOMS OF DIABETES

- Passing urine more regularly, especially at night
- Increased thirst
- Extreme tiredness
- Genital itching or regular episodes of thrush
- Slow healing of wounds
- Recurring infections such as boils
- Blurred vision
- Weight loss, usually in people with Type 1 diabetes

People with Type 1 diabetes produce no insulin and therefore require insulin injections as well as a healthy diet and regular physical activity in order to manage their diabetes.

Type 2 diabetes develops when your body can still make some insulin but not enough, or when the insulin that is produced doesn't work efficiently enough. It usually occurs in people over 40 years old, though in people of South Asian and African Caribbean origin, it often appears after the age of 25. However, recently more children are being diagnosed with the condition. Type 2 diabetes is treated with a healthy diet and increased physical activity. Tablets and/or insulin may also be needed.

RISK FACTORS FOR TYPE 2 DIABETES INCLUDE

- A family history of diabetes
- Being overweight and inactive or with a waist measurement over a certain size (see page 16)
- Ethnic origin – South Asian and African Caribbean people are more at risk
- Gestational diabetes (diabetes during pregnancy)

To find out more, visit www.diabetes.org.uk/measureup

THE INSULIN CONNECTION

When you eat food, some of that food is broken down into glucose (sugar) during digestion. The glucose then flows into the bloodstream where it is circulated around the body and subsequently used up by your muscles. As soon as glucose enters the blood, a signal goes to your pancreas gland to allow your body to release the hormone insulin. Insulin helps glucose to move from your blood into your muscles or liver where you can use it for energy or store it for later use.

Blood glucose is normally very carefully controlled by insulin. But in Type 1 diabetes, no insulin is produced and in Type 2 diabetes, not enough is produced or the insulin produced is not working properly (this is called insulin resistance) and often your blood glucose level will rise above the normal range. The aim of eating well and having a healthy, active lifestyle is to help to keep blood glucose within a healthy range. Diabetes UK currently recommends that people with diabetes aim to keep their blood glucose levels at 4-6 mmol/l before meals and at no higher than 10 mmol/l two hours after meals.

The good news is that you can help to manage your blood glucose levels in Type 2 diabetes by making small, simple changes to your lifestyle. In both types of diabetes, the main aim is to achieve healthy blood glucose levels as well as blood pressure and cholesterol that is as near normal as possible. This, together with a healthy lifestyle, will improve well-being and protect against long-term damage to the eyes, kidneys, nerves and major arteries. Being overweight makes diabetes control more difficult as excess weight makes it hard for the body to use insulin properly. Losing weight will help diabetes control for both Type 1 and Type 2.

Since people with diabetes are more prone to heart problems, it is especially important to reduce the risk of heart disease by stopping smoking if you smoke, and monitoring blood pressure and blood fat levels. A healthy lifestyle and losing weight can significantly reduce your cardiovascular risk.

The plan

No doubt you've tried many other diets – and no doubt the weight
has just crept back on again. This is a classic pattern for people who
get sucked into quick-fix diets. But the good news is that by making
sustainable changes to your lifestyle today, you can live a full life. The
key here is the word 'sustainable'. And no change in your behaviour is
going to last if it means making drastic changes to your day-to-day
habits. And that is why this plan is right for you:

■ You love your food! You're tempted by the enticing photographs and you
enjoy and savour your meals. With this plan, you can have your cake and eat
it. Every recipe has been created with good health and a balanced diet in
mind, and the menus have been designed to help you lose weight slowly and
steadily while indulging in your favourite foods. A weight loss plan can only
succeed in the long term if you enjoy it.

■ Every recipe has been carefully analysed and the ingredients used are in
accordance with healthy eating recommendations. Simply keep to the portion
sizes and cooking methods suggested; this will help to ensure that you are
having a healthy balance of foods that are low in saturated fat and that
contain slowly digested carbohydrates that help to keep your blood glucose
levels steady throughout the day.

■ We suggest regular meals and healthy snacks, so you really don't feel you're
on any sort of diet! This isn't about restriction, it's about enjoyment. And
when you're eating regularly, you're more likely to be performing at your best
and to have good energy levels throughout the day. Now that must be good
for your self-esteem too!

■ This plan includes healthy low glycaemic index (GI) foods such as beans,
lentils, whole grains, nuts, seeds, pasta and plenty of fruits and vegetables.
Since these foods can take longer to digest, they can help you feel fuller for
longer while keeping your blood glucose levels steady.

■ This is not a quick-fix diet and the menu plans do not cut out any food
groups. It's simply a way to kick-start a healthy balanced lifestyle, appropriate
for the whole family.

■ All in all, the simplicity and attractiveness of this plan means that you're
more likely to keep to it.

Weight-watching, why bother?

Around 80 per cent of people who have Type 2 diabetes are overweight, and it's likely that they carry this excess weight around their waist. This extra weight causes the body's insulin to be less effective, creating a greater risk of developing diabetes. So if you already have diabetes and are overweight, then losing weight, especially from the tummy area, will improve your body's sensitivity to insulin, which will make it work more effectively. And if insulin works better, your blood glucose is likely to be under better control. Good news all round!

BENEFITS OF WEIGHT LOSS

- Improves blood glucose levels
- Lowers blood pressure
- Lowers unhealthy blood fats (triglycerides, LDL – low-density lipoprotein or 'bad' cholesterol)
- Reduces risk of long-term complications of diabetes
- Improves mobility
- Gives you a sense of well-being and improves your self-esteem

THE LOWDOWN ON BLOOD GLUCOSE

Diabetes is a condition where blood glucose is abnormally high, so it doesn't take a genius to work out that any steps that help to keep blood glucose levels within a healthy range will improve the overall control of diabetes. When you eat carbohydrate foods such as bread, potatoes, rice and sugary foods, they are digested into glucose which then passes into the bloodstream. If you have diabetes, the insulin in your body is less able to transport the glucose from the blood into your muscles where it can be used for energy. So if you have undiagnosed diabetes, your blood glucose remains high.

Losing weight, even small amounts of weight, together with a healthy diet and physical activity, will help to improve how sensitive you are to insulin (see The 10 Per Cent Factor, page 18). And by watching what and when you eat, you will be able to influence the rise and fall in your blood glucose levels. This, in turn, will improve your 'glycaemic control', which simply means that it will help to minimise fluctuations in your blood glucose levels. This way, you will be less likely to suffer the symptoms of highs and lows in your blood glucose and this can improve your long-term health.

Your diabetes medication should match the food you eat and your level of activity. As you lose weight and become more active you become less resistant to insulin your body produces or that you inject, therefore whether you have Type 1 or Type 2 diabetes you may need to have your diabetes medication dose reduced. Some people with Type 2 diabetes who lose weight as a result of their lifestyle changes are able to control their diabetes with less or without any diabetes medication. Diabetes is a lifelong condition and their diabetes hasn't been cured, but it has been controlled through food and physical activity. As Type 2 diabetes is a progressive condition, medication may be needed in the future to control your blood glucose levels.

HOW CAN I TELL IF I NEED TO LOSE WEIGHT?

In this book, we give you simple, practical steps on how to lose weight gradually and keep it off, but for now let's establish how much weight you need to lose in order to make a significant improvement to your health.

Calculate your BMI

(Reproduced with kind permission from Jacqui Troughton, Advanced Diabetes Practitioner, Leicester Royal Infirmary, UHL (www.leicestershirediabetes.org.uk)

Your body weight as well as your shape is likely to affect your health. The body mass index (BMI) is used internationally by health professionals to assess whether your weight could be putting your health at risk. You can work this out by taking your weight in kilograms and dividing it by your height in metres squared. This means that if you weigh 80kg and are 1.9m tall, your BMI will be 22.1 (80 ÷ [1.9 x 1.9] = 22.1).

HEALTH RISK ASSOCIATED WITH BODY MASS INDEX (BMI)

	BMI	BMI (Asian origin)	Health Risk
Underweight	Less than 18.5	Less than 18.5	
Normal	18.5-24.9	18.5-22.9	
Overweight	25-29.9	23-24.9	Increased
Obese	30.0-34.9	25.0-29.9	High
	35.0-39.9	30.0-34.9	Very High
Morbidly obese	Greater than 40	Greater than 35	Extremely High

If you fall into the overweight, obese or morbidly obese categories, your weight is putting your long-term health at risk, so by reading this book, you are taking your first steps to doing something about it.

HOW DO YOU SHAPE UP?

Although your weight is a very useful indicator of long-term health, more and more research is pointing to the importance of where your fat is distributed and how that can have significant effects on health. Carrying too much weight around the middle or central obesity (also sometimes referred to as apple-shaped) can increase the risks of developing heart disease and high blood pressure. There is extensive research to show that people who are centrally obese tend to be less sensitive to the effect of insulin. This can then lead to a condition called insulin resistance and people who have insulin resistance tend to be more prone to developing diabetes. People with diabetes are likely to already be less sensitive to insulin and so if your excess weight is carried around your middle, it is particularly important to take steps now. As you can see from the waist circumference guidelines below, you do not need to be very apple-shaped to be at increased risk.

If you carry your weight on your hips rather than on your waist, you are likely to be pear-shaped, and this is a less detrimental way to carry excess fat. But the most important measurement is your waist and you should work towards meeting the guidelines below. You can do this by eating a range of healthy foods within a calorie-controlled diet and by engaging in regular physical activity.

MEASURING YOUR WAIST CIRCUMFERENCE

By measuring your waist you can get a good idea if you have excess fat around your waist. Stand with your feet hip distance apart and take the measurement between the top of the hip bone and the lowest rib. The tape needs to be snug but it shouldn't compress the skin and needs to be parallel to the floor. Breathe out before the waist measurement is taken.

WHAT SIZE DO YOU TAKE?

A study published in the *Journal of Human Nutrition and Dietetics* in 2005 looked at clothing size and whether this might be a parameter in assessing health risks. Some 200 men and 160 women took part in a research project in Glasgow. Detailed measurements such as waist circumference, BMI and blood pressure were taken.

The BMI score is the standard marker for describing obesity in populations, but in clinical practice, waist circumference measurement is a more accurate method of predicting risk. High-waist circumference and BMI values as indicated below and on page 15 were found to be strongly linked to clothing size. What's especially fascinating (and useful) is that the cut-off points for increased health risk related to UK waist size were 34 trousers for men and a UK dress size of 14 for women. 'High risk' cut-offs were size 36 trousers for men and a dress size of 16 for women.

The bigger the sizes in your wardrobe, the greater the risk of heart disease – in the research study, trousers over waist size 38 in men indicated a nearly four-fold chance, and women with a dress size above 18 had a seven-fold chance of having at least one of the main cardiovascular risk factors.

WAIST MEASUREMENT	INCREASED HEALTH RISK
White and African-Caribbean men	94cm (37in) or above
Asian men	90cm (35in) or above
All women	80cm (31.5in) or above

The 10 per cent factor

You know that your goal in managing your diabetes is to keep blood glucose levels steady throughout the day and in the long term. This will help to prevent the long-term complications of diabetes such as heart, eye and kidney problems. Minimising fluctuations in your blood glucose levels can also help your day-to-day health and improve the quality of your life as you begin to feel better both physically and mentally. Eating well throughout life makes good sense, and it's not about setting yourself unrealistic weight loss targets. The best news is that, if you are overweight, by losing just 5-10 per cent of your weight, you can make a major contribution to improving the quality of your long-term health.

THE SCIENCE BIT

The dietary guidelines in this book are based on scientific evidence. We have interpreted the research for you and translated it into practical advice. There is extensive research to show that if you are overweight, losing weight leads to a significant improvement in your blood glucose levels and there are no two ways about it. What's interesting is that there is now research to show that losing just 10 per cent (based on someone weighing 100kg losing 10kg) carries considerable health benefits.

There is good evidence to suggest that in people who need to lose weight, a moderate weight loss of 5-10 per cent of body weight will have a major impact on the long-term complications of obesity. Weight reductions of 5-10kg in someone who weighs 100kg have been shown to improve back and joint pain, as well as symptoms of breathlessness.

A large study, called the UK Prospective Diabetes Study (UKPDS), carried out over a 20-year period on more than 5,000 people with Type 2 diabetes, was published in the *Lancet* in 1998. The results showed that, in people who weighed 100kg, weight loss of 10kg can achieve greater reductions in HbA1c (the longer-term predictor of how well your blood glucose is doing) and fasting blood glucose than treatment with the diabetes medication metformin alone. For people with diabetes, the weight loss also reduced the need for blood pressure and lipid-lowering treatment (medication to lower blood cholesterol and triglyceride). These findings don't necessarily mean that you would not need treatment any more if you were to lose weight, but that you need to check with your healthcare team.

A comprehensive review of studies on weight reduction of 10 per cent or less was published in the *International Journal of Obesity* in 1992. The studies indicated that in obese people with Type 2 diabetes, a 10 per cent weight loss appeared to improve blood glucose control and reduce blood pressure and cholesterol levels. Modest weight reduction also appeared to increase length of life.

A recent UK study on overweight and obese adults published in the *British Medical Journal* suggested that a weight loss of 10 per cent was possible and reasonable over 6-12 months and had beneficial effects on health.

Changing your diet, activity levels and losing weight could help to reduce the dosage of your diabetes medication.

If you are overweight, even a 5 per cent loss of body weight can improve insulin action, decrease fasting blood glucose concentrations, and reduce the need for diabetes medications. Data from the Diabetes Prevention Program (DPP) published in the *New England Journal of Medicine* in 2002 demonstrated that weight loss (of 7 per cent in the first year) and increased physical activity (150 minutes of brisk walking per week) was nearly twice as effective as drug treatment with metformin in preventing diabetes in people who already had raised blood glucose levels.

Participants in the Diabetes and Obesity Intervention Trial (DO IT, conducted by the University of Pittsburgh) who achieved a 10 per cent weight loss after six months were able to match the weight loss of another group of people who also took a weight loss drug (Orlistat). In fact, 18 out of 25 people who were taking diabetes medication at the start of the study were able to stop taking their medication! We obviously cannot guarantee that you can expect these results; remember that people in a research study are carefully monitored so that they keep to the dietary and physical activity changes recommended. However, anyone who is overweight can benefit from losing just 10 per cent of their body weight. And that's a fact.

In short, if you lose 10 per cent of your body weight, for instance by reducing your weight from 100kg to 90kg, you could enjoy the following health benefits:

- Improved blood glucose levels
- Lower blood cholesterol and triglycerides (types of blood fats)
- Reduced blood pressure
- Less back and joint pain
- Reduced risk of angina
- Less breathlessness
- Improved sleep
- Improved self-esteem and confidence

For many people with diabetes, changing their diet and activity levels and/or losing weight could help to reduce the dosage of diabetes medication required, so you will need to liaise with your healthcare team before and during your weight loss programme.

If you are able to improve your insulin sensitivity (and this amount of weight loss should certainly help to do that), then you will have a better chance of keeping your blood glucose levels under control and hence this may help you to reduce the amount of diabetes medication you currently take. If you are not on any diabetes medication, then any weight loss will certainly help to reduce your need for it in the future.

Are you really ready?

No doubt you've tried diets in the past. If you've had a diagnosis of diabetes in the family, you may have been motivated to eat more healthily. If you simply wanted to lose weight for your looks, no doubt you've tried various diets which have had short-term results. So what's different this time? This book is not about another diet - it's about healthy eating. But first things first: this section will enable you to explore how motivated you are today, and this will help you to gauge whether you are really ready to take on this healthy lifestyle. You will lose weight only if you make sustainable changes to your normal everyday habits - what you eat and how active you are.

GETTING STARTED: WEIGHT-LOSS MOTIVATION ASSESSMENT

Try the quiz below to see how motivated you are. It will help to assess how important weight loss is to you, at this particular stage in your life. Weight loss is important to me because:

FOR MY HEALTH

My doctor says I should ☐

I think it would improve my symptoms ☐

I don't want my health to get worse ☐

I need to lose weight before an operation ☐

FOR PERSONAL REASONS

Because activity makes me breathless ☐

Because I have difficulty with dressing/undressing ☐

Because I can't fit into seats in planes, buses ☐

Because I can't keep up with my partner/children ☐

To set an example for children/grandchildren ☐

To have more energy to enjoy life ☐

FOR EMOTIONAL REASONS

To feel better about myself ☐

To have more control over my life ☐

To make someone else happy ☐

Because I am embarrassed about being overweight ☐

FOR MY APPEARANCE AND SOCIAL LIFE

I think I will look better ☐

Others want me to look better ☐

I will be able to wear nicer clothes ☐

To be more attractive to my partner ☐

To improve job opportunities ☐

To feel able to enjoy a normal social life ☐

You may have other reasons, so use the space below to remind yourself:

_____

_____

_____

_____

If your reasons for losing weight are mainly to do with other people, for example your doctor, partner or friend then this can be less helpful than if they are important to you personally. If weight loss is more important to you than to others then you are more likely to succeed – as you are if you have the support of other people.

Once you have identified your reasons for wanting to lose weight, it can be helpful to think about the following questions:

1 Why do I want to lose weight now?

2 What would be the good things about making changes in order to lose weight? (e.g. I will have more energy)

3 What would be the more challenging aspects about making changes in order to lose weight? (e.g. I don't enjoy exercise and will have to do more)

4 What would be the good things about staying as I am? (e.g. no effort is needed)

5 What would not be good about staying as I am? (e.g. the arthritis in my knees will get worse)

Spending time giving some thought to these questions could be very helpful because you will have a more realistic idea about your motivation and the things that might get in the way of success. If, for example, you have a long list of answers to questions 3 and 4, then it is possible that your motivation is low at the moment. However, if you have a long list of answers to questions 2 and 5, then your motivation is probably high.

Questions 3 and 4 will help you see any barriers to losing weight. If there are practical difficulties to overcome, you can work on solutions to these with your dietitian or practice nurse.

WILLPOWER BOOSTERS

■ If you think something is going to be difficult to achieve, it will be! This time, see your new healthy lifestyle plan as something to be embraced; something that you really want here, today, now, as you know it will have benefits for you and your family.

■ If you find that you have a bad day in terms of your food or activity choices, simply acknowledge the lapse and start again. You don't need to wait till Monday to get back on track!

■ Make a list of all the benefits you will achieve once you have lost weight successfully and kept it off. Keep this list handy to remind yourself.

■ Think about how your self-confidence may change once you have lost the weight.

■ Will you be any different at work when you achieve your goals?

■ How will being healthier affect your relationships and how you behave around people whom you care about?

If you feel after having done this quiz that you are not ready to take on a weight loss plan, then let it go, wait a while and come back and review this when you feel more ready. Trying to lose weight if you are not really ready can often be counter-productive.

Guidelines for the weight loss diet

Our eating plan is based on national recommendations for healthy eating. However, it is no substitute for personalised dietary advice for diabetes. If you have been diagnosed with diabetes, it is imperative that you visit a registered dietitian for advice that is tailored to your needs. If you have not already seen a registered dietitian, ask your GP to refer you to one at the local hospital or GP clinic. He or she will be able to assess your current eating habits and help you with specific advice to improve the control of your diabetes and also to lose weight. Always speak to your GP before embarking on any weight loss plan.

1 EAT THREE REGULAR MEALS

Avoid skipping meals and spread your breakfast, lunch and evening meal over the day. This will not only help you control your appetite but also assist in controlling your blood glucose levels. Another associated benefit of this control is that it will help to improve your mood and concentration.

This plan encourages you to eat breakfast, lunch and dinner, with light snacks in between. We have designed the plan so that you are in total control of what you eat and also so that you are able to enjoy really tasty home-cooked foods.

Remember that extra snacks can pile on the pounds so choose low-calorie ones like fruit or low-fat yogurt where possible. There is also a chapter of recipes for healthy home-made snacks.

For some people who take diabetes medication, snacks are essential – check with your healthcare team if this applies to you. It is also important to talk to your healthcare team as it may be possible to adjust your diabetes medication so that you don't need to snack between meals.

The other important thing about eating regularly is that it will actually prevent you from reaching for the cookie jar because you will find that you are less hungry. There is research to show that eating small, regular meals can help to keep your blood glucose levels stable and even help you to consume fewer calories.

2 EAT MORE FRUIT AND VEGETABLES

OK, so you've heard it all before. Despite the fact that the Food Standards Agency and the British Dietetic Association have run campaigns on promoting the importance of eating at least five fruit and vegetables a day, current intakes in the UK are still averaging around three portions. All of us, whether we have diabetes or not, should aim for at least five portions a day, but many people are confused by exactly how much a portion is.

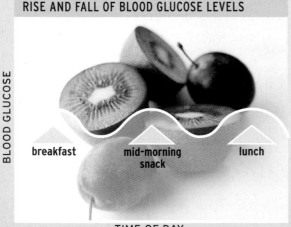

RISE AND FALL OF BLOOD GLUCOSE LEVELS

BLOOD GLUCOSE

breakfast   mid-morning   lunch
             snack

TIME OF DAY

Here are some examples of a portion:
- Medium-sized fruit, such as an apple, banana or orange
- 1 large slice melon or pineapple
- 2 plums, apricots, satsumas or kiwi fruit
- Handful of grapes or cherries
- 3 tablespoons fresh fruit salad or tinned fruit in natural juice
- ½ a grapefruit or avocado
- 1 tablespoon dried fruit, such as raisins, apricots
- 1 glass (150ml) unsweetened fresh fruit juice (counts only once as one of your five a day)
- 3 tablespoons raw or cooked vegetables
- 1 dessert bowl of salad
- 3 heaped tablespoons beans and pulses (count only once as one of your five a day)

You will notice that a large majority of the recipes in this book have some fruit or vegetables as part of the ingredients list, which will help to count towards your five a day.

Remember also that fruit and vegetables are nature's power foods. They are rich in a wide range of vitamins and minerals and in fibre, and they are also low in fat and calories. In short, as part of a weight loss plan, they are your best friends. In terms of disease prevention, there is extensive research to show that eating more fruit and vegetables can reduce your risks of developing heart disease, some types of cancer and gut problems.

3 INCLUDE STARCHY CARBOHYDRATE FOODS WITH EACH MEAL

People with diabetes are advised to choose foods that help to keep their blood glucose levels steady. This includes eating carbohydrate or starchy foods (bread, pasta, chapatis, potatoes, yam, noodles, rice and cereals) that are digested and absorbed as glucose into the bloodstream.

The amount of carbohydrate you eat is important in the control of your blood glucose levels. All varieties of carbs are fine but try to include those

THREE KEY POINTS ABOUT FRUIT AND VEG

- Eat a wide range of different coloured fruit and vegetables. By ensuring you have a good variety, you are more likely to get a wide range of nutrients. For example, orange-coloured apricots, papaya and carrots will provide the antioxidant beta-carotene, while red tomatoes will provide cancer-protective lycopene.

- Potatoes don't count, because they are considered to be a starchy carbohydrate food and they don't have the range of nutrients you would normally find in fruit and vegetables. Beans and pulses (see above left) do count, but only as one portion.

- Fresh, frozen, tinned, dried and juiced fruit and vegetables all count, so look for different ways to include them in your diet – a glass of juice for breakfast, a spoonful of dried fruit over your cereal and, of course, vegetables with every meal.

that are more slowly absorbed (i.e. have a lower glycaemic index) as these won't affect your blood glucose levels as quickly. Diabetes advice has always focused on choosing low glycaemic index (GI) carbohydrates, but since 2004 the GI has hit the headlines for its successful results for weight loss and its overall health benefits.

Essentially the GI is simply a measure of how quickly foods that contain carbohydrate raise your blood glucose levels. If you have diabetes, eating more foods containing slowly absorbed carbohydrates can help to even out blood glucose levels. There are extensive tables listing GI values of foods. However, it is not necessary for you to know individual GI values. What's important is that you choose those foods that will offer glycaemic benefits, that is, slow steady rises in your blood glucose level after meals.

Using GI on its own is not appropriate, as you also need to think about how much carbohydrate you're eating. Your blood glucose is determined by both the quality of the carb (GI) and its quantity. The glycaemic load (GL) is calculated by taking the percentage of a food's carbohydrate content per portion and multiplying this by its GI value. It gives you a more accurate indication of how your blood glucose will be affected by a particular serving of food, so it is a reflection of both the quality and quantity. This is helpful when thinking about foods with a high GI, like watermelon. Although it has a high GI rating, a slice is actually quite low in carbohydrate. So the GL of a serving of watermelon is low and this is a perfectly acceptable food. Focusing on the GL on its own is not appropriate for diabetes, because it is possible to follow a low GL diet by simply eating less carbohydrate – and these carbs could be high GI. Research suggests that the link between low GL diets and good blood glucose levels is the consumption of low GI foods, not low carbohydrate intake. In short, you don't need to get bogged down by GI figures or GL; simply eat those carbs that offer you the best blood glucose response, and watch your portion sizes.

GI TIPS FOR DIABETES

■ Eat regularly. How nice does that sound?

■ Make sure you eat three meals a day. Breakfast is really important as it helps to steady your blood glucose after the overnight fast. If you ensure you choose a low GI breakfast, you're less likely to be tempted by unhealthy snacks later.

■ Choose at least one low GI carbohydrate (see opposite page) at every meal, and ideally at snack times, but remember to watch portion sizes to keep the GL low.

■ Get into the habit of piling vegetables onto your plate. For weight loss, half your plate should be filled with vegetables. In the other half, fill two thirds with starchy food like rice, pasta and potatoes and fill the final third with low-fat protein foods like lean meat, fish, beans, low-fat cheese, Quorn or tofu.

■ Base your desserts on fruit. You will find a tempting array of fruity endings to your meals in this book.

■ A little careful planning goes a long way. Scan our list of healthy low GI foods and keep some handy. You'll find that our snack recipes are great for a quick pick-me-up.

■ The effect of a low GI meal can run into the following meal, which helps keep blood glucose more even during the whole day.

■ Make sure you eat more vegetables. And if they are lightly cooked, they are likely to be more slowly digested, which will help with your glycaemic control. You'll end up doing more chewing, which will make you feel more satisfied, and because your plate will look fuller, this will make you feel you're eating more.

All great psychological tips to enhance your motivation!

Lower GI Choices

BREADS

Choose granary, seeded, multi-grain, rye, soya and linseed. Wholemeal bread and white bread are both considered to be high GI foods because the flour is more refined and this makes the bread more quickly digested and absorbed. The key is to choose foods that need more chewing, so granary bread with the whole wheat grains intact will offer you a far better blood glucose result than wholemeal or white bread. And eating it with lower GI foods (such as baked beans) will be even better.

OTHER STARCHY ACCOMPANIMENTS

Basmati rice, brown rice and some varieties of long-grain rice (such as easy cook) offer a medium GI rating. Sticky rices such as jasmine and risotto tend to make blood glucose rise more quickly. With any type of rice, try to cook it until just tender rather than mushy.

Most types of pasta do very well on the GI scale. Choose pasta regularly and cook till al dente because if it is overcooked, it will have a higher glycaemic index. Remember though to keep to the amounts given in the recipes in this book, and to team it up with other low GI accompaniments like a side salad.

Potatoes tend to have a higher GI rating, especially if mashed or overcooked. Choose new boiled potatoes in their skins or try sweet potatoes. This doesn't mean that mashed potatoes are off the menu – simply team them up with a low GI food such as baked beans or coleslaw in a reduced-calorie dressing.

Experiment with different types of grains. Bulgur, quinoa, oats and couscous are all excellent choices.

PULSES

Beans and lentils, such as kidney beans, butter beans, chickpeas and red and green lentils are fantastic and count once a day as part of your five fruit and vegetables recommendation. Try adding them to stews, casseroles and soups or to a salad.

FRUIT AND VEGETABLES

Most fruit and vegetables offer a low GI rating, so enjoy them regularly. Whenever possible, have them raw and whole rather than cooked.

GO FOR LOW GI FOODS AS PART OF A BALANCED DIET

One of the reasons why GI has not been taken up extensively is that the research as it currently stands is based on the blood glucose response after eating a single food. So, for example, we know that the GI value of wholemeal bread is high when it is eaten on its own. However, we don't normally do that. As soon as you put some ham and salad into a wholemeal bread sandwich, you lower its consequent GI value and hence its effect on your blood glucose. Also your glycaemic load will be different depending whether you eat one or two slices – two slices will have a greater effect on your blood glucose levels.

If your diet doesn't include many low GI foods, you could end up with more highs and lows in your blood glucose levels, which is not desirable. This is why it's really important to include as many low GI carbohydrates in your diet as possible. And if you can, choose those low GI foods that are fresh and natural, like porridge, beans and lentils, pasta and so on, because you'll know that you're also getting a good range of nutrients.

4 BE FAT-WISE

Weight for weight, pure fat has more than twice the calories of pure protein or carbohydrate. So, it makes sense to eat less fat if you want to lose weight. You may think low-fat food is boring, but there is a wide array of herbs, spices, low-fat marinades and more that can add zest and taste to low-fat dishes – just check out the recipe for Indonesian king prawn curry (page 88) if you need reassurance.

Research from the Mediterranean countries shows that people who eat diets rich in mono-unsaturated fats such as olive oil, avocados, nuts and seeds do seem to have lower risks of heart problems. Obviously, there is more to this than just the type of fat eaten, and other lifestyle and cultural factors will be at play. However, it is fine to enjoy small amounts of monounsaturated oil in cooking and that's what you'll be doing when you try out our mouth-watering dishes.

Choose lower-fat cooking methods such as baking, grilling, poaching and roasting without fat. You may enjoy some low-fat manufactured foods, such as fat-free dressings, low-fat spreads, lower-fat sausages and so on. These are all fine as part of a healthy balanced diet; however, you will find that the recipes in this book will provide you with less processed yet tasty dressings and treats that are also low in fat. And a great trick is to make your own spray oil using olive or rapeseed oil. Simply invest in a pump spray bottle (available from most good household stores) and pour your favourite oil into the bottle. This way you are likely to use less oil when spraying from a bottle than when pouring. Or use a brush dipped in oil to lightly coat your ingredients or pan.

TYPES OF FAT

Fats are an essential component of the diet, but too much of certain types can lead to a build-up of fatty streaks in the arteries, which can reduce blood flow to the heart. One of the main risk factors of coronary heart disease is high blood cholesterol. If you eat foods that cause your blood cholesterol to rise, you're more likely to suffer from heart problems.

There are two types of cholesterol in the blood:
■ **high density lipoprotein** (HDL) represents 'good' cholesterol – the higher your HDL, the lower your risk of heart disease;
■ **low density lipoprotein** (LDL) is often called 'bad' cholesterol – a high LDL level can increase your risks as it leads to the formation of fatty deposits in the arteries.

Certain types of fat will have an effect on your HDL and LDL levels. Remember that it's firstly important to cut down on the amount of fat you eat. Within this, aim in particular to reduce those foods that are rich in saturated fat, as this is linked to heart disease. Choose unsaturated fats or oils, especially monounsaturated fat found in olive oil and rapeseed oil, as these types of fat reduce LDL blood cholesterol. Saturated fat and trans fat do the opposite, so cut down on foods that contain these (see below).

■ Saturated fats. Usually found in fatty meat, full-fat dairy products, butter and lard, ghee, coconut oil and palm oil.
■ Trans fats. These are found in some processed foods such as cakes, biscuits, pies and pastries. You may see them listed on an ingredients list as hydrogenated vegetable fats.
■ Monounsaturated fats. Found in olive oil and rapeseed oil and spreads based on these oils. Although these are healthier fats, it's still important to watch your overall fat intake.
■ Polyunsaturated fats. Include sunflower oil, corn oil and soya oil, and margarine and spreads based on these oils. These have been shown to lower blood cholesterol levels and therefore help in reducing the risk of heart disease, but, weight for weight, all fats and oils have the same number of calories, so it's still important to limit amounts. Oily fish contain polyunsaturated fats that are essential for your well-being as your body cannot make them.

5 GET YOUR OMEGAS

Oily fish is rich in a particular type of essential fat called omega 3. These fish oils have been shown to be protective against heart disease because they help to reduce blood stickiness and can also help to reduce a particular type of blood fat, called triglycerides. Aim to eat at least two portions of oily fish a week. Examples include salmon, trout, herring, tuna, mackerel, pilchards and sardines but tinned tuna does not contain any of these good fats as they are destroyed in the tinning process.

6 DON'T PASS THE SALT!

High blood pressure makes you more prone to heart conditions. Since eating too much salt is linked with high blood pressure, and people with diabetes are more at risk of high blood pressure, cutting down on salt makes a whole lot of sense.

Salt is the common name for sodium chloride and it is the sodium part of salt that is harmful if taken in excess. It's estimated that people in the UK eat at least 10g or 2 teaspoons of salt each day, but adults should limit their salt intake to 6g or less a day (just over a teaspoon). Most of the salt you eat comes from processed food, and it is very likely that you are taking in far more than this amount each day, especially if you rely heavily on processed meals and snacks.

GET SALT SMART

■ Measure the amount of salt you add in cooking and gradually cut down the amount you use. The recipes in this book allow you to taste the natural flavours as added salt is kept to a minimum.

■ Avoid adding salt at the table. Choose pepper, paprika and other spices instead.

■ Experiment with herbs and spices, using for example freshly ground spices, dried and fresh herbs, paprika and freshly ground black pepper and you won't miss the taste of salt.

■ For varied flavours, try lemon and lime juice, balsamic vinegar and tabasco.

■ Choose products that have a reduced-salt content, for example tuna tinned in spring water rather than brine, and unsalted butter and reduced-salt condiments.

■ Cut down on salty foods such as salted crisps, nuts, savoury biscuits and salty pastries. Choose fresh fruit, unsalted nuts and unsalted popcorn as alternative snacks.

■ Salted and smoked foods such as bacon, sausages, smoked fish, some tinned fish and other processed convenience foods are often loaded with salt. Whenever possible, use fresh foods such as fish, lean meat, fruit and fresh vegetables. They only have a small amount of salt present naturally.

■ Read food labels carefully. Salt may appear as sodium, sodium chloride, mono-sodium glutamate or bicarbonate of soda.

7 LIMIT THE SWEET STUFF

Eating well doesn't mean saying goodbye to sugar. Sugar can be used in foods and in baking as part of a healthy diet. However choose squashes and fizzy drinks that are sugar-free, have no added sugar or are labelled 'diet' as sugary drinks cause blood glucose levels to rise quickly.

8 ALCOHOL

It is recommended that women drink no more than two units of alcohol a day and men no more than three units. If you are watching your weight, remember that alcohol contains empty calories. It is best to limit your alcohol intake to about one unit a day and to have a few alcohol-free days a week. One unit of alcohol is equivalent to half a pint of normal-strength beer or lager, or a pub measure (25ml) of spirits, but in recent years the alcohol content of most pub-sized measures has gone up. You might find that a pint of premium lager now contains as much as three units of alcohol, and a glass of wine (175ml) as much as two units.

Try alternating your alcoholic drink with a diet soft drink, or making your drink go further by adding sparkling water or having spirits in a tall glass made up with one measure and a diet soft drink. Also, try to have eight glasses of fluid each day, including water, tea, coffee, sugar-free drinks and squashes.

Never drink alcohol on an empty stomach, as it can cause hypoglycaemia (low blood glucose levels) if you are taking certain diabetes medication. And remember never to drink and drive.

9 DIABETIC PRODUCTS – WHO NEEDS THEM?

Steer clear of any foods labelled specifically for people with diabetes. They tend to be expensive and often contain just as much fat or calories as standard versions of the same food. What's more, the types of sweetener used in these products may have a laxative effect and can still affect your blood glucose levels.

Shop till you drop...
...a waist size that is!

Shopping for food is good; the more you shop for food, hopefully the less you will rely on takeaways. It's what goes into your trolley that might need a closer look. No doubt the recipes in this book will entice you into buying choice ingredients that will help you to savour your food and enjoy a range of healthy meals. This section will give you further guidance on how to make speedy yet sensible supermarket choices.

Reading a label may not be the most attractive pastime when you're rushing around trying to buy tonight's dinner. So here are some very quick tips to help you be a little bit more discerning as you scan the shelves.

1 A LITTLE OR A LOT?

Nutritional information given on food packaging can be used to tell whether a food has a little or a lot of fat, salt, fibre or sugar. The table below shows you how to do this. You will often see nutritional information displayed as per serving and per 100g. The 'per 100g' value is useful if you want to compare two similar products, such as ready-made sauces, to see which is healthier. For foods that you eat frequently or in large amounts it is more appropriate to use the nutrition information given per serving.

HOW TO TELL IF A PRODUCT CONTAINS A LITTLE OR A LOT OF A PARTICULAR NUTRIENT

This is a lot (per 100g)	This is a little (per 100g)
10g of sugars or more	2g of sugars or less
20g of fat or more	3g of fat or less
5g of saturated fat or more	1g of saturated fat or less
3g of fibre or more	0.5g of fibre or less
0.5g of sodium or more	0.1g of sodium or less
1.25g of salt or more	0.25g of salt or less

2 GREEN FOR GO!

It's important to think about how a food fits into the overall balance of your diet. The Food Standards Agency has introduced a new traffic light labelling system to help you do this, to appear initially on convenience-type food. The red, amber and green coding will show at a glance whether the level of four key nutrients (fat, saturated fat, sugar and salt) in 100g of a product is high, medium or low.

Red = High
Amber = Medium
Green = Low

So, if you see a 'red light' on the front of the pack, you know the food is high in something we should be trying to cut down on. It's fine to have that food occasionally, but try to keep an eye on how often you choose these foods, or try eating them in smaller amounts. If you see amber, you know the food isn't too high, and it's fine to go for this most of the time, but whenever you can, try to find one that has a green code. The more 'green lights', the better the choice.

Since packaged foods are made up of lots of ingredients, you will find that the traffic light

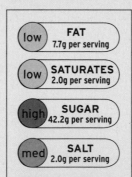

labels will often have a combination of greens, ambers and reds. If you're comparing two brands, go for the one that has more green and amber and, just like when you're driving, try to avoid the one with the most red lights.

Surveys of consumers show that sales of unhealthy foods have begun to go down since the traffic light scheme was introduced and hopefully this will encourage more manufacturers to introduce healthier alternatives.

You can see traffic light labelling in many supermarkets on a range of foods. More manufacturers and retailers are also introducing the traffic light scheme.

3 GDA

Guideline Daily Amounts (GDAs) were developed by the IGD which is a food and grocery industry research organisation. GDAs are guidelines for healthy adults and children about the approximate amount of calories, fat, saturated fat, carbohydrate, total sugars, protein, fibre and salt required for a healthy diet.

GDAs are only intended for groups of people rather than specific individuals, because individuals vary in so many ways in terms of their size and lifestyle. However, GDAs are a useful measure to show how much of a particular nutrient you get in a serving of food. Some manufacturers have developed a new GDA labelling system, which is displayed on the front of packaging.

The GDAs are meant to act as a guide and help you to compare products. The illustration below is an example of the labelling on food packaging.

GUIDELINE DAILY AMOUNTS (GDAs) EXPLAINED

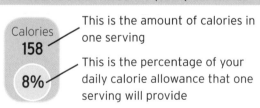

Calories
158

This is the amount of calories in one serving

8%

This is the percentage of your daily calorie allowance that one serving will provide

What are the Guideline Daily Amounts?

Calories	2000
Fat	70g
Saturated Fat	20g
Salt	6g or less
Sugar	90g
Fibre	24g

In this way, you could compare the amount of calories per serving, for example, against the GDAs. This system has been taken up by some of the large manufacturers and supermarkets.

4 FANCY A TOUR?

Some supermarkets run shopping tours led by a registered dietitian. They last about an hour and visit different sections of the store, looking at healthy choices for people wanting to manage diabetes and lose weight. You can learn how to understand the information given on food labels and how to compare products to make healthy choices. Ask the store manager or your local community dietitians if diabetes store tours are available in your area.

What participants have said about diabetes store tours...

- I've had diabetes for ten years and thought I knew it all, but this has really opened my eyes.
- It's really good being able to see all the choices available to me where I normally shop.
- I enjoyed learning to read labels and choose healthier foods.
- This will make eating healthily much easier – there is so much variety to choose from.
- I liked learning from other people's experience on the tour.
- I will vary my diet and include more healthy choices.

If there are no tours in your area you can still increase the variety of your diet and make healthy choices by reading food labels or by checking the traffic light or GDA information. Or you could take a virtual tour. The Diabetes UK website (www. diabetes.org.uk) will guide you through a store tour in the comfort of your armchair.

Lastly, remember that your shopping trolley should ideally be filled with more whole foods than processed foods. Check out the Lower GI Choices section (page 25) for some quick tips on what to buy and see overleaf for some more ideas.

■ Choose reduced-sugar/low-sugar foods and sugar-free drinks when shopping. When buying foods containing sweeteners, choose those with intense sweeteners. These used to be known as artificial sweeteners, e.g. saccharin (E954), aspartame (E951), acesulfame potassium (E950), cyclamates (E952) and (E955) sucralose. If you do use sweeteners, choose a variety.

■ Avoid 'diabetic' products that contain nutritive sweeteners (sorbitol, maltitol, mannitol, isomalt, xylitol) as these have no more benefit to people with diabetes than ordinary ones. Diabetic products can be just as high in fat and calories as ordinary versions and therefore can still affect your blood glucose level. Furthermore, these sweeteners can have a laxative effect if eaten in excess.

■ On food labels, the list of ingredients is always given in descending order of amount. The higher up an ingredient is on the list, the more of that ingredient is contained in the food.

■ Be aware that there may be several types of fat, sugar or salt in the ingredients list – hydrogenated vegetable oil, corn oil, cocoa butter and milk fat are all types of fat; sucrose, invert sugar syrup and molasses are all types of sugar. Salt content may be listed as salt or sodium chloride, and salt is present in MSG (monosodium glutamate) and stock.

■ If possible, take a detour so you don't need to pass the chocolate/confectionery aisle and the snacks sections. And it's best not to shop when you're hungry as the sight and smell of bakery goods might be a little too challenging to resist!

■ You may be less tempted by unhealthy choices if you make a shopping list and stick to it.

FAT-O-METER

Amount of saturated fat found in different types of cheese – based on a serving

Highest in saturated fat

Cream cheese

Parmesan

Brie

Edam

Cheddar cheese
reduced fat

Mozzarella
reduced fat

Ricotta

Feta
reduced fat

Cottage cheese, plain

Quark

Lowest in saturated fat

SALT-O-METER

Amount of salt found in different types of snacks – based on a serving (portion weight given in brackets)

Snacks highest in salt

Tortilla chips (50g)

Bombay mix (30g)

Cornflakes (35g)

Reduced-salt crisps (30g)

1 low-salt crispbread (10g)

Plain unsalted popcorn (75g)

1 unsalted cracker (7g)

Unsalted nuts (25g)

Fruit and vegetable crudités (80g)

Snacks lowest in salt

SUGAR-O-METER

Amount of sugar (total) found in different types of snacks – based on one serving

Highest in sugar

Milk chocolate bar

Reduced-fat sponge cake

Jam doughnut

Cereal chewy bar

Fruit scone

Teacake

1 slice Fruit malt loaf

1 Jaffa cake biscuit

1 Rich tea biscuit

Lowest in sugar

TIPS FOR HEALTHY EATING OUT

■ Avoid bar nibbles such as peanuts, crisps and so on.

■ When ordering food, ask for any sauce or dressing to be left off or served on the side.

■ Order extra portions or large portions of vegetables/salads - and of course bread rolls (ideally grainy bread) if your meal doesn't have enough carbohydrate for your needs - or if your meal is delayed.

■ Ask if portions of salad/vegetables can be substituted for less healthy options.

■ Avoid ordering fried foods, dishes with pastry and dishes with creamy sauces. Go for tomato-based sauces instead.

■ Order skinless chicken or ask for the skin to be taken off. If it comes to your table with the skin on, just remove it neatly and set aside. You will reduce the calories in your meal by doing this.

■ Leave some food on your plate. Ask the waiter to remove your plate as soon as you have finished so you are less likely to pick at any leftover food.

■ If you have wine with a meal, dilute it with sparkling water or alternate it with diet soft drinks.

■ Choose a fruit-based dessert.

Move more!

You don't need to go to the gym or jog every day in order to start becoming more active. Just incorporate the 'move more' strategy into your everyday life. Moving more simply means standing up to change the channel on your TV rather than reaching for the remote, it means going upstairs to get one thing immediately rather than waiting till you need three or four things, it means getting up from your desk to refill your water or coffee. Every little action you take will have a cumulative effect on your daily energy expenditure and the more you increase your expenditure, the more effective your weight loss is likely to be. But before you start any new activity, talk to your doctor – especially if you are taking any medication for diabetes or heart disease; have any complications of diabetes such as foot or eye problems; are not sure which activities suit you; or have any conditions that may restrict your mobility or ability to be active.

IT'S A SIMPLE EQUATION:

If the food you eat (energy taken in) is less than the amount you expend (energy used up), you will lose weight. Your aim is to achieve a calorie or energy deficit.

Physical activity isn't just about weight loss. Take a look at this list of additional benefits of increasing your activity levels:

- Improves your diabetes control and helps to prevent some of the complications of diabetes
- Improves muscular strength and increases flexibility
- Prevents and manages high blood pressure
- Reduces lower back pain and strengthens the back
- Helps to reduce anxiety, tension and stress
- Increases self-esteem and confidence
- Supports maintaining a balanced and healthy diet
- Helps to beat the blues
- Helps to keep up a healthy body image and good sex life
- Improves your cholesterol levels
- Helps with weight management
- Reduces the risk of heart disease, osteoporosis and cancer

Physical activity is often linked with a healthy self-image and it can, with a little practice, become second nature. The key is to choose an activity you enjoy and that fits in with your lifestyle! If much of your day is spent behind a desk, or in a stuffy environment, you may well feel lethargic and tired. Believe it or not, injecting some physical activity into your day can actually make you feel fresher and more energised. So moving around, ideally in the fresh air, can have a beneficial impact on your mood. Think about doing some activity as soon as you finish work or at home, as soon as you get in. Even ten minutes makes a difference.

The recommended **minimum** amount of activity for adults is 30 minutes on at least five days of the week. If you're normally inactive and are now keen to build up your stamina and fitness levels, it's best to seek advice from your GP. Otherwise, gradually build more movement into your daily routine. Here are some ideas:

- First have a goal. It's only when you have a target that you will be really motivated. You could choose to have a daily or weekly aim, but make it realistic and specific and write down how you will make it happen. For example, 'I will go for a brisk walk for 20 minutes three times a week.'

■ Think of household chores and gardening as your ways to increase your energy expenditure and aim to make them more vigorous (for instance, moving furniture to vacuum underneath, or mow the lawn or get an allotment).

■ Carry shopping bags to your car rather than using a trolley. Or park the car further away from the supermarket.

■ Walk or cycle to work.

■ Try activities with the family, such as swimming, bowling, cycling, a walk or a game of football in the park.

■ Do simple exercises while watching TV or listening to music (gentle jogging on the spot, stretches, lunges, abdominal exercises, pelvic floor exercises, contracting your buttocks, etc).

■ Make an appointment with yourself to exercise on a weekly/daily basis and make sure you keep your appointment! To help keep yourself motivated, keep a record of your progress, gradually build on this and make a note of how it makes you feel afterwards. Treat yourself (with something other than food) if you are keeping to your goal. Set ongoing rewards for your achievements – a new CD, a glossy magazine or a new book when you've achieved a step towards your goal.

Exercise log

WEEK:

Goal/aim for this week:
e.g. walk to work three times a week, use the stairs instead of the lift

DATE	TYPE OF ACTIVITY *e.g. walking*	EXERCISE TIME *e.g. 20 minutes*	DISTANCE *e.g. 1km*	ANY COMMENTS
Total time of exercise				

About the recipes

These recipes have all been specially created and nutritionally balanced so at first you will want to follow them exactly – and so you should! However, don't be afraid to alter them slightly by substituting one herb for another. There's also a wealth of different grains, beans and pastas so do experiment.

Hopefully, all the ingredients in these recipes are available in your local supermarkets. Having said that, they all do have different ranges of products so you may have to shop around to some extent. An occasional trip to a health food shop is also well worthwhile. In some cases we have been quite specific about an ingredient. We recommend:
- brown flour with malted grain
- multi-grain or granary bread

IN YOUR STORE-CUPBOARD, KEEP A STOCK OF...

- tins of beans in WATER – without added salt or sugar
- tins of chopped tomatoes
- jars or tins of roasted red peppers – always drain and rinse well before use
- dried pasta – try alternatives such as wholewheat, spelt and kamut
- brown rice – particularly brown basmati
- noodles – rice, rice and quinoa, buckwheat (soba)
- grains – couscous, quinoa, pearl barley, wholewheat grains or spelt grains (faro) and bulgur wheat
- porridge oats
- seeds – linseed, hemp, pumpkin, sunflower or sesame
- dried fruits – raisins, apricots or prunes
- nuts – almonds, pine nuts and hazelnuts, but choose the natural varieties which are unsalted

IN YOUR FREEZER, KEEP...

- peas
- soya beans
- broad beans
- spinach
- sweetcorn

- free-range, organic eggs
- semi-skimmed milk
- yogurt – 0% fat Greek yogurt or natural fat-free
- olive or rapeseed oil
- citrus fruits – unwaxed where possible

READ THE LABEL – IT'S QUITE AN EYE OPENER!
- Don't assume that all 'light' cheeses have the same number of calories.
- Check the salt content of 'low-fat' or 'extra-lean' products – often salt is added as a balance to the loss of flavour from the natural fats in the meat.

TRICKS OF THE TRADE
- Invest in a fine (microplane) grater – parmesan goes a long way when it's finely grated.
- Slice meats thinly.
- Use a smaller plate (eat slowly and chew well).

COOKING
- Use non-stick pans wherever possible and a light spray of oil as necessary.
- Add a splash of water to stop ingredients sticking.
- Grill, steam or bake wherever possible.

BUTTER
This appears very occasionally in this book. It's a natural product and we prefer to use it in our recipes to give the best results and flavour. You may prefer to use a polyunsaturated (PUFA) or a monounsaturated (MUFA) spread to replace the butter. If so, use it in equivalent quantities to the specified amount of butter; however do be aware that it may give a slightly different result.

BREADS
Note that salt levels are usually much higher in commercially prepared breads so as often as possible do try to make your own (see pp49 & 66).

About the menu plans

Welcome to your tailored and tasty menu plans. Our Weight Loss Plan has been designed to help you lose weight slowly and steadily, at the rate of about $\frac{1}{2}$ to 1kg (1–2lb) per week. This is followed by a sensible Weight Maintenance Plan, which will help you to maintain a healthy weight.

Each day has been carefully designed to help ensure a balanced amount of carbohydrate and other nutrients, whilst keeping your fat, salt and sugar intake within acceptable limits. There is no need for you to worry about doing any calculations; these have all been done for you.

YOUR MENU GUIDELINES

1 Plan ahead so that you have the ingredients ready for making your meals each week.

2 The menu plans run for seven days, but this doesn't mean that you need to eat exactly the same food every week; it is simply an example of how you can achieve an appropriate calorie intake.

3 The weight maintenance recipes have been given a special logo as they are slightly higher in calories and more appropriate for the time when you have achieved your target weight.

4 If you are losing more than 1kg (2lb) a week on the Weight Loss Plan, or still losing weight on the Weight Maintenance Plan, then it is better for you to eat a little more to slow down your weight loss. Think about having extra fruit, low-fat yogurt, lower-fat milk or carbohydrate such as seeded bread, basmati rice or pasta to supplement the menu plan.

5 You need three servings of calcium-rich foods daily. This has been taken into consideration when devising the menu plans, although if you prefer to swap the snacks or desserts for low-fat yogurt or a skinny latte, then this will help you to achieve your daily targets. Any milk listed separately in the menu plans is in addition to the milk allowance.

6 You can bulk out your meals with extra vegetables except beans, pulses, sweetcorn, peas and root vegetables. Also allowed are tea, coffee,

other drinks made with milk (from the allowance) and artificial sweetener; diet soft drinks, low-cal squashes, sugar-free sparkling water and mixers.

7 Alcoholic drinks have been included in the menu plans. It's important to keep to the limits as described on page 28, but the calorie contribution from alcohol has been included in both plans. This will allow you to have four units of alcohol a week during the Weight Loss phase and ten units a week during the Weight Maintenance phase.

Although calorie needs for men and women do vary, these plans are based on 1500 kcalories for the Weight Loss phase and 2000 kcalories for the Weight Maintenance phase. If you are a moderately active man or active woman, you may wish to allow extra snacks or larger portions during both phases. This is not intended as a weight-reducing diet for children; however the recipes are healthy, delicious and appropriate for children. You may wish to give active children larger portions and extra healthy snacks.

Weight loss plan

MONDAY	TUESDAY	WEDNESDAY
Breakfast Quick banana sandwich (p49)	**Breakfast** Banana and cinnamon porridge (p44) with fruit	**Breakfast** Tropical fruit tabbouleh (p44)
Mid-morning snack Dill and buttermilk roll (p66)	**Mid-morning snack** Apricot beaker loaf, 1 slice (p68)	**Mid-morning snack** Chilli bean pâté (p67) with celery sticks
Lunch Bean and salad wrap (p94) **Dessert** Mango fool (p140)	**Lunch** Smoked trout kedgeree (p83) **Dessert** 200g berries and 150ml low-fat yogurt	**Lunch** Curried veg and lentil soup (p76) **Dessert** Afghan milk jelly (p133)
Mid-afternoon Oat thin (p81) and milky drink (150ml lower-fat milk)	**Mid-afternoon** Spiced seed mix (p61) and 200ml fat-free fromage frais	**Mid-afternoon** 2 Digestive biscuits (p61)
Dinner Asian calf's liver (p126) **Dessert** Anna's iced berry crush (p130)	**Dinner** Steak with beans and greens (p106) **Dessert** Souffléed pumpkin pie custard (p130)	**Dinner** Spiced cod (p105) **Dessert** Roasted peaches with blueberries (p138)
Bedtime Hot chocolate nightcap (p73)		**Bedtime** Hot chocolate nightcap (p73)
Milk for the Day 300ml skimmed or 200ml semi-skimmed	**Milk for the Day** 300ml skimmed or 200ml semi-skimmed	**Milk for the Day** 300ml skimmed or 200ml semi-skimmed
Alcohol none	**Alcohol** none	**Alcohol** none

THURSDAY	FRIDAY	SATURDAY	SUNDAY
Breakfast Hedgerow yogurt (p49)	**Breakfast** Banana and strawberry smoothie (p48)	**Breakfast** Hedgerow yogurt (p49)	**Breakfast** Spiced tomato and bacon toasts (p50) and fresh fruit
Mid-morning snack Prune and hazelnut 'salami' (p65)	**Mid-morning snack** 2 Soft hazelnut chews (p58)	**Mid-morning snack** Banana lolly (p58)	**Mid-morning snack** Warm popcorn (p70)
Lunch Beetroot, potato and apple salad (p83) **Dessert** Low-fat yogurt and a pear	**Lunch** Vegetable soup (p79) **Dessert** Strawberry tart (p137)	**Lunch** Indonesian king prawn curry (p88) **Dessert** Seared pineapple with pomegranate salsa (p134)	**Lunch** Panzanella salad (p79) **Dessert** Basmati rice pudding (p140)
Mid-afternoon 4 Mini seed snacks (p62)	**Mid-afternoon** Oat thin (p81) and milky drink (150ml lower-fat milk)	**Mid-afternoon** Spiced seed mix (p61) with pot of low-fat yogurt	**Mid-afternoon** Apricot beaker loaf, 1 slice (p68)
Dinner White bean and lamb stew (p109) **Dessert** Summer berry fruits (p130)	**Dinner** Noodles with chicken, prawns, squid (p121) **Dessert** Papaya and lime sorbet (p133)	**Dinner** Spaghetti with courgettes, ricotta, basil & lemon (p101) **Dessert** Stove-top plums (p138)	**Dinner** Sunday pot roast (p124) **Dessert** Anna's iced berry crush (p133)
	Bedtime Hot chocolate nightcap (p73)		**Bedtime** Hot chocolate nightcap (p73)
Milk for the Day 300ml skimmed or 200ml semi-skimmed	**Milk for the Day** 300ml skimmed or 200ml semi-skimmed	**Milk for the Day** 300ml skimmed or 200ml semi-skimmed	**Milk for the Day** 300ml skimmed or 200ml semi-skimmed
Alcohol none	**Alcohol** 175ml wine + sparkling water	**Alcohol** 25ml spirit + low-cal mixer	**Alcohol** 25ml spirit + low-cal mixer

Weight maintenance plan

MONDAY

Breakfast
Quick avocado sandwich (p49) and fresh fruit

Mid-morning snack
Indian-style cottage cheese (p67) with red pepper batons

Lunch
More than a mouthful tomato soup (p95)
Dessert
Mango fool (p140)

Mid-afternoon
Banana loaf (p73)

Dinner
Tuna, pink grapefruit and avocado salad (p114)
Dessert
Basmati rice pudding (p140)

Evening snack
Hot chocolate nightcap (p73)

Milk for the Day
As before

Alcohol
2 units

TUESDAY

Breakfast
Super slices (p50) with fresh fruit

Mid-morning snack
Date and rhubarb wedge (p68)

Lunch
Spicy bean jacket potato (p89)
Dessert
Spiced seed mix (p61) and 150ml fat-free fromage frais

Mid-afternoon
Roasted soya beans (p70) and a small glass of fresh fruit juice

Dinner
Tomato, tofu cocktail (p61)
Penne with artichokes (p100)
Dessert
Pears in nightshirts (p134)

Evening snack
Hot chocolate nightcap (p73)

Milk for the Day
As before

Alcohol
none

WEDNESDAY

Breakfast
Mother grain porridge (p48) with 1 slice bread (p49)

Mid-morning snack
Soft cheese dip with apple (p65)

Lunch
Avocado dip and tomato wedges (p90)
Dessert
Strawberry tart (p137)

Mid-afternoon
Date and tahini dip (p65)

Dinner
Asian meatballs (p127)
Dessert
Fresh berries with rosewater foam gratin (p137)

Evening snack
2 Mini seed snacks (p62)
Hot chocolate nightcap (p73)

Milk for the Day
As before

Alcohol
2 units

THURSDAY	FRIDAY	SATURDAY	SUNDAY
Breakfast Hedgerow yogurt (p49) with 1 slice oat, soya and linseed bread (p49)	**Breakfast** Mediterranean breakfast plate (p54)	**Breakfast** Boiled eggs with 'asparagus' soldiers (p53)	**Breakfast** Mushrooms on toast (p54) with fresh fruit
Mid-morning snack A pint of prawns (p66)	**Mid-morning snack** Digestive biscuit (p61)	**Mid-morning snack** Apricot beaker loaf, 1 slice (p68)	**Mid-morning snack** Spiced seed mix (p61) and 150ml low-fat yogurt
Lunch Mixed grain, seed and herb salad (p93) **Dessert** 150g blueberries and 150ml fat-free fromage frais	**Lunch** Asian chicken and lettuce rolls (p95) **Dessert** Stove-top plums (p138)	**Lunch** Cauliflower rarebit (p90) **Dessert** Afghan milk jelly (p133)	**Lunch** Low-GI pizza (p93) **Dessert** Fresh figs with rosewater foam gratin (p137)
Mid-afternoon Red lentil bar (p71)	**Mid-afternoon** Prune and hazelnut 'salami' (p65)	**Mid-afternoon** Spiced seed mix (p61) and pot of low-fat yogurt	**Mid-afternoon** Apricot and pistachio 'salami' (p65) and a small glass of fresh fruit juice
Dinner Trout in a pea and artichoke stew (p113) **Dessert** Bacoffee pots (p140)	**Dinner** Poached salmon and tahini sauce (p116) **Dessert** Basmati rice pudding (p140)	**Dinner** Grilled chicken with spinach and lentils (p118) **Dessert** Apple galette (p138)	**Dinner** Paillard of venison (p122) **Dessert** Roasted peaches with blueberries (p138)
Evening snack 2 Digestive biscuits (p61)	**Evening snack** 2 Oat thins (p58)	**Evening snack** 2 Soft hazelnut chews (p58)	**Evening snack** Hot chocolate nightcap (p73)
Milk for the Day As before	**Milk for the Day** As before	**Milk for the Day** As before	**Milk for the Day** As before
Alcohol 2 units	**Alcohol** 2 units	**Alcohol** 2 units	**Alcohol** none

breakfast

This meal is crucial for your blood glucose levels and will set you up for the day. It is also a great opportunity to eat one or two portions of fruit and veg and our recipes will help you do this. We have also included a recipe for an oat, soya and linseed bread that is specified in other recipes – but where we have listed a soya and linseed bread, we suggest using Vogel – as photographed here.

banana and cinnamon porridge

A sustaining twist on a classic favourite. Leftovers will keep in the fridge for 1-2 days; reheat the porridge with a little extra water, either in the microwave or on the hob.

SERVES 6

- **200g porridge oats with bran**
- **½ teaspoon ground cinnamon**
- **4 medium bananas**
- **2 tablespoons clear honey**
- **300g strawberries, hulled and halved**

1 Bring 1 litre water to the boil in a large saucepan then pour in the porridge oats, stirring all the time until well mixed. Stir in the cinnamon.
2 Bring to a simmer, then simmer gently for about 10 minutes, adding extra water if liked to give a soft consistency. Stir occasionally.
3 Roughly mash three of the bananas and stir through the porridge. Remove from the heat and stir in the honey.
4 Slice the remaining banana and mix with the strawberries. Spoon the porridge into bowls and serve at once, topped with the fruit.

PER SERVING: 221 kcals; 3g fat; 0.5g saturated fat; 45g carbohydrate; 0.01g sodium

tropical fruit tabbouleh

Tabbouleh is made with bulgur or cracked wheat and is normally a savoury salad with loads of parsley, mint, garlic and tomatoes, but for those wanting a sweet version that ticks the healthy eating boxes, give this one a go! It is best to make this the night before as it needs a couple of hours to soak and rest, but it will keep, covered, in the fridge for 3-4 days.

SERVES 4

- **25g golden caster sugar**
- **4 cardamom pods, lightly crushed**
- **1 small bunch mint**
- **pulp from 4 passion fruits**
- **finely grated zest and juice of 2 unwaxed limes**
- **150g bulgur wheat**
- **175g prepared pineapple, diced**
- **1 kiwi fruit, diced**
- **1 pomegranate, peeled and seeds separated**
- **1 small banana, thinly sliced**
- **1 papaya, de-seeded and diced**

1 Put the sugar in a small saucepan with 300ml water, the cardamom pods, half the mint, all the passion fruit pulp and the lime zest. Bring slowly to the boil, then simmer gently for 5 minutes.
2 Put the bulgur wheat in a large bowl and strain the hot syrup over it, squeezing out all the juice from the pulp left in the sieve. Cover and leave for up to 1 hour until the grains have swelled and absorbed all the liquid.
3 Pick the reserved mint leaves from the stalks and chop them finely. Stir into the bulgur wheat along with the lime juice and all the prepared fruit. Cover and allow the flavours to develop for 1 hour if possible.

PER SERVING: 249 kcals; 1g fat; 0.1g saturated fat; 58g carbohydrate; 0.01g sodium

citrus fruit salad

Goji berries, oval red berries grown in China, are considered to be one of the most nutritionally rich fruits available. Dried goji berries are available in health food shops.

SERVES 2
- 2 pink or red grapefruit
- 2 oranges
- 4 clementines
- 2 tablespoons dried goji berries or sultanas
- 2 x 150g tubs low-fat natural yogurt

1 Using a small serrated knife, peel the grapefruit and oranges, removing all the white pith. Squeeze any juice from the trimmings and reserve.
2 Carefully remove the segments of fruit from the membrane that holds them in place. Squeeze the trimmings once more to collect all the juice.
3 Peel the clementines and cut horizontally in thin slices. Mix all the fruits with the reserved juices and the goji berries, or sultanas, and serve with the yogurt.

PER SERVING: 237 kcals; 2g fat; 1g saturated fat; 47g carbohydrate; 0.13g sodium

oriental eggs

Something a little different for breakfast, quick to make and satisfying to eat. As this recipe is low in carbohydrate, make sure you have a carb-rich snack before lunch – the dill and buttermilk roll on page 66 would be perfect or a slice or two of seeded bread with a little reduced-calorie jam.

SERVES 4
- 1 teaspoon rapeseed oil
- 1 teaspoon sesame oil
- ½ red pepper, cut in 1cm dice
- 2 spring onions, sliced
- 50g button mushrooms, quartered
- 25g beansprouts, rinsed and dried
- 6 medium eggs
- 2 teaspoons fish sauce (nam pla)
- 1 teaspoon reduced-salt soy sauce
- freshly ground white pepper
- 4 slices soya and linseed bread, toasted

1 Heat the oils in a non-stick frying pan or wok over medium heat and cook the red pepper, spring onions and mushrooms for about 2 minutes until softening, then add the beansprouts and cook for a further 1 minute.
2 Meanwhile, beat the eggs with the fish sauce, soy sauce and a little pepper, then pour over the vegetables and stir, drawing the sides in as you would for scrambled eggs until the eggs are set to your liking.
3 Serve immediately, with the toast.

PER SERVING: 245 kcals; 13g fat; 3g saturated fat; 18g carbohydrate; 0.66g sodium

mother grain 'porridge'
with sunshine fruits

Quinoa (pronounced keen-wah) was one of the most sacred foods of the Incas - they called it 'mother grain' because of its nutritious qualities (though it's a seed rather than a grain). It can be used in both sweet and savoury dishes. This porridge will keep in the fridge for 2-3 days.

SERVES 4

- **125g quinoa**
- **250g fat-free natural yogurt**
- **150ml semi-skimmed milk**
- **1 tablespoon clear honey**
- **1 large papaya**
- **1 large mango**
- **4 passion fruits**

1 Rinse the quinoa well in a sieve under running cold water then transfer to a medium-sized saucepan with 300ml boiling water from the kettle. Stir well then cover and simmer for 10 minutes.

2 Remove from the heat and leave to go cold. Put the quinoa in a bowl and loosen the 'grains' with a fork. Stir in the yogurt, milk and honey.

3 Prepare the papaya and mango and cut in bite-size pieces. Halve the passion fruits, remove the seeds and pulp and combine with the papaya and mango.

4 Spoon the 'porridge' into bowls and top with the fruit.

PER SERVING: 228 kcals; 3g fat; 0.5g saturated fat; 44g carbohydrate; 0.09g sodium

banana and
strawberry smoothie

Try to choose locally grown strawberries wherever possible - they will have so much more flavour than imported ones.

SERVES 2

- **2 large bananas**
- **100g strawberries, hulled**
- **2 tablespoons fat-free natural yogurt**
- **200ml semi-skimmed milk**
- **1 tablespoon clear honey**
- **1 tablespoon wheatgerm**
- **12 ice cubes**

Place all the ingredients in a liquidiser goblet and blend until smooth. Serve at once.

PER SERVING: 228 kcals; 3g fat; 1g saturated fat; 46g carbohydrate; 0.06g sodium

oat, soya and linseed bread

This dense loaf freezes well, but slice it first.

MAKES 18 SLICES
- **200g porridge oats**
- **50g soya beans, coarsely ground**
- **250g brown bread flour with malted wheatgrain**
- **1 sachet (6-7g) easy blend yeast**
- **1 teaspoon salt**
- **2 tablespoons linseeds**
- **1 teaspoon rapeseed oil, to grease a 900g loaf tin**

1 Mix the porridge oats with 200ml cold water. Cover and leave to soak for at least 2 hours.

2 Combine the remaining ingredients and add to the soaked oats with about 150ml hand-hot water. Mix to a firm, but not sticky dough. Turn out onto a lightly floured surface and knead for 2 minutes.

3 Shape to fit the prepared loaf tin and press down gently. Cover loosely with a plastic bag and leave in a warm place to rise for 2-3 hours until the dough has reached the top of the tin and has a slightly domed surface.

5 Preheat the oven to 220°C/425°F/gas mark 7 and bake for about 45 minutes until the loaf is risen and firm and sounds hollow when tapped on the base. Cool on a wire rack.

PER SLICE: 105 kcals; 2g fat; 0.3g saturated fat; 17g carbohydrate; 0.11g sodium

SERVING SUGGESTION
Banana sandwich - mash half a small banana and sandwich between 2 slices.
Avocado sandwich - squash a quarter of a medium avocado and a teaspoon of Worcestershire sauce between 2 slices of bread.

BANANA SANDWICH - PER SERVING: 246 kcals; 4g fat; 1g saturated fat; 43g carbohydrate; 0.22g sodium

AVOCADO SANDWICH - PER SERVING: 330 kcals; 16g fat; 2g saturated fat; 36g carbohydrate; 0.28g sodium

hedgerow yogurt

Whole wheat 'berries' and spelt grains are available in health food shops. Soak them overnight then drain and cook in fresh boiling water for 30-35 minutes until tender. Drain and use in salads or in this fruity mixture. This yogurt will keep in the fridge for 1-2 days.

SERVES 2
- **½ vanilla pod, split**
- **2 x 150g tubs 0% fat Greek yogurt**
- **250g blackberries**
- **2 dessert apples, cored and grated**
- **50g cooked wheat berries or spelt grains**

Scrape the seeds from the vanilla pod and mix with the yogurt. Fold in the blackberries, grated apple and wheat, and serve.

PER SERVING: 251 kcals; 1g fat; 0.1g saturated fat; 44g carbohydrate; 0.12g sodium

super slices

FOR WEIGHT MAINTENANCE

Perfect for a quick breakfast - do have the yogurt and apple as well. If you don't trust yourself to limit the portion then store in an airtight container in the freezer!

SERVES 6

- 50g dried dates, chopped
- 75g brown bread flour with malted wheatgrain
- 2 teaspoons baking powder
- 2 teaspoons ground mixed spice
- 50g ready-to-eat dried apricots, chopped
- 50g walnut pieces, chopped
- 25g sunflower seeds
- 50g cut mixed peel, rinsed and dried
- 1 egg, beaten with 4 tablespoons semi-skimmed milk
- 6 x 150g tubs low-fat natural yogurt
- 6 small dessert apples

1 Preheat the oven to 180°C/350°F/gas mark 4. Line the base and sides of a 450g loaf tin with baking paper.

2 Put the dates in a small saucepan with 4 tablespoons water and simmer for about 5 minutes until softened. Leave to cool.

3 Mix the flour, baking powder and spice in a large bowl then stir in the rest of the dry ingredients. Add the cooled date purée, egg and milk and mix until evenly combined.

4 Transfer to the prepared tin and level the surface. Bake for about 35 minutes until risen and firm to the touch. Cool slightly then remove from the tin and leave to cool on a wire rack. When cold cut into 6 thick chunks (or 12 - 2 per portion - or 18 - 3 per portion - thin slices) and serve each portion with a pot of yogurt and an apple.

PER SERVING: 332 kcals; 11g fat; 2g saturated fat; 47g carbohydrate; 0.37g sodium

spiced grilled tomato and bacon toasts

Spice up your breakfast a little with these indulgent tomatoes, but make sure you eat a large orange as well to get a good range of nutrients.

SERVES 4

- 8 plum tomatoes, halved lenthways
- 1 teaspoon light muscovado sugar
- 2 teaspoons mild or medium-hot curry powder
- ¼ teaspoon freshly ground black pepper
- 2 teaspoons olive oil
- 4 reduced-fat smoked bacon medallions, finely diced
- 4 slices soya and linseed bread, toasted
- 4 large oranges, as an accompaniment

1 Preheat the grill to high. Arrange the tomato halves cut-side up on a baking tray. Mix together the sugar, curry powder and pepper and sprinkle over the cut surface of the tomatoes.

2 Drizzle each with a few drops of oil then grill for 8-10 minutes until the tomatoes are soft but not collapsed.

3 Sprinkle the diced bacon over the tomatoes and return to the grill for 2-3 minutes.

4 Put four halves of tomatoes on each slice of toast and serve immediately.

PER SERVING: 244 kcals; 6g fat; 1g saturated fat; 37g carbohydrate; 0.56g sodium

boiled eggs
with asparagus 'soldiers'

This is my version of a classic recipe. Not for every day as it is higher in calories than the other breakfasts in this chapter, but perfect for a special treat!

SERVES 1

- 250g bundle asparagus, trimmed (about 170g trimmed weight)
- 2 medium eggs
- freshly ground black pepper or smoked paprika, to sprinkle
- 2 slices oat, soya and linseed bread (see page 49), to serve

1 Steam or cook the asparagus in boiling water for 5-7 minutes, depending on the thickness of the stalks. The stalks should be tender but still with a 'bite' (al dente). Drain thoroughly.
2 Meanwhile, cook the eggs in simmering water for 3-5 minutes depending on your personal preference: 3 minutes will give a very lightly cooked egg, 4 minutes will give a fairly firm white and a runny yolk, 5 minutes will give a firm white and a lightly cooked yolk.
3 Serve the eggs and asparagus at once, with ground black pepper or smoked paprika to sprinkle, and the bread cut into 'soldiers'.

PER SERVING: 398 kcals; 16g fat; 4g saturated fat; 38g carbohydrate; 0.31g sodium

roast tomatoes
with field mushrooms and chickpeas

A dish that can be prepped in advance and popped in the oven when you are ready to eat. Serve with a glass of fresh orange juice.

SERVES 2

- 4 beefsteak tomatoes
- 1 tablespoon extra virgin olive oil
- 1 garlic clove, finely diced
- ½ small onion, finely diced
- 250g field or flat mushrooms, roughly chopped
- 4 tablespoons tinned chickpeas, drained and rinsed
- 1 teaspoon thyme leaves, finely chopped
- freshly ground black pepper
- 2 slices wholemeal bread, toasted

1 Slice off the top of each tomato, about 1cm down, and set aside. With a teaspoon, paring knife or melon baller, scoop out the seeds and central core of the tomato, being careful not to split the sides of the tomato. Discard the seeds.
2 Heat the ollve oil in a frying pan then add the garlic and onion and cook over a low heat until the onions have softened but not coloured. Remove the onions and garlic and set aside.
3 In the same frying pan, cook the mushrooms over a high heat until they have started to wilt. Stir in the onion mix and the chickpeas, and season with thyme and black pepper.
4 Preheat the oven to 200°C/400°F/gas mark 6. Fill the tomato cases with the mushroom mixture and replace the tops of the tomatoes. Set the 4 tomatoes on a roasting tray and cook in the oven until the tomatoes have softened but not split (about 15-20 minutes). Serve immediately with the toast and orange juice.

PER SERVING INCLUDING JUICE: 284 kcals; 9g fat; 1g saturated fat; 43g carbohydrate; 0.24g sodium

mushrooms
on toast

This is great for brunch or breakfast; the flavours of each part of the dish really come together.

SERVES 2

- 1 teaspoon sesame oil
- 1 garlic clove, crushed
- 1 green chilli, de-seeded and finely chopped
- 3cm piece of fresh ginger, peeled and grated
- 350g button mushrooms, halved
- 1 tablespoon reduced-salt soy sauce
- 1 teaspoon clear honey
- 2 heads bok choi, shredded
- 4 spring onions, sliced
- 1 tablespoon sesame seeds
- freshly ground black pepper
- 4 slices oat, soya and linseed bread (see page 49), toasted, to serve

1 Heat the sesame oil in a large non-stick frying pan. Add the garlic, chilli and ginger and cook for 30 seconds, stirring constantly.
2 Add the mushrooms and cook for 2 minutes, stirring from time to time, until lightly golden.
3 Stir in the soy sauce, honey, bok choi and spring onions and cook for a further 3 minutes, stirring occasionally. Add a splash of water if necessary to prevent sticking. Stir in the sesame seeds and season with black pepper.
4 Serve immediately, with the toast.

PER SERVING: 330 kcals; 11g fat; 2g saturated fat; 43g carbohydrate; 0.80g sodium

mediterranean
breakfast plate

Throughout much of the southern Mediterranean you may see this on the breakfast menu. Make sure the tomatoes are at room temperature for the best flavour.

SERVES 3

- 4 large tomatoes, cut in wedges
- 200g cucumber, cut in chunks
- 150g reduced-fat feta-style cheese, cut in thin slices
- 9 black olives
- 2 teaspoons olive oil
- freshly chopped marjoram, to sprinkle
- freshly ground black pepper, to sprinkle
- 6 slices oat, soya and linseed bread (see page 49), to serve

Arrange the tomatoes, cucumber, cheese and olives on three plates. Sprinkle with olive oil, marjoram and pepper and serve with the bread.

PER SERVING: 355 kcals; 13g fat; 4g saturated fat; 41g carbohydrate; 1.04g sodium

snacks

These healthy nibbles are perfect to bridge the gaps between meals - there's even a luxurious hot chocolate to enjoy just before bedtime. Make up a batch of a couple of recipes so you will have a store to hand, but be sure not to eat them all in one go.

soft hazelnut chews

These lovely bites make a great tea-time snack.

MAKES 12 CHEWS
- **100g shelled hazelnuts**
- **40g golden caster sugar**
- **½ teaspoon natural vanilla extract**
- **2 egg whites**

1 Preheat the oven to 180°C/350°F/gas mark 4. Put the hazelnuts on a baking tray and roast to a golden brown colour – about 15 minutes. Increase the oven temperature to 200°C/400°F/gas mark 6. Line a baking tray with baking paper.
2 Put the nuts and sugar in a food-processor and pulse, then add the vanilla and 1 of the egg whites and pulse to a paste.
3 Whisk the remaining egg white until stiff and fold in the nut mixture. Spoon 12 dollops well spaced on the baking tray and spread each one a little. Bake for 10-15 minutes until golden.
4 Leave to cool a little then transfer to a cooling rack until cold. Store in an airtight container. Freeze if preferred.

PER SERVING: 70 kcals; 5g fat; 0.4g saturated fat; 4g carbohydrate; 0.01g sodium

oat thins

These crisp biscuits are almost irresistible, so store these in the freezer then you can get ONE out as a snack either mid-morning or afternoon.

MAKES 12 THINS
- **90g porridge oats**
- **75g unrefined light muscovado sugar**
- **2 tablespoons brown bread flour with malted wheatgrain**
- **2 egg whites, lightly beaten**
- **2 tablespoons unsalted butter, melted**

1 Preheat the oven to 190°C/375°F/gas mark 5. Line a large baking tray with baking paper.
2 Mix all the ingredients together. Spoon 12 dollops well spaced on the baking tray, then, using a fork, flatten each one to about 8-9cm diameter.
3 Cook for 15-20 minutes until golden brown. Leave to cool on the tray then transfer to a wire rack until cold and crisp. Store in an airtight container. Freeze if preferred.

PER SERVING: 81 kcals; 3g fat; 1g saturated fat; 13g carbohydrate; 0.01g sodium

banana lollies

The simplest recipe to make, but a delicious snack to have in the freezer.

SERVES 4
- **2 large bananas**

Peel each banana and cut in half crossways. Push a lollipop stick into the cut end then wrap in clingfilm and freeze until required.

PER SERVING: 71 kcals; 0.2g fat; 0.1g saturated fat; 17g carbohydrate; 0g sodium

spiced seed mix

A portion of these, with a glass of water, will stave off hunger pangs. Measure out each portion separately so you don't over-indulge.

SERVES 12

- **75g pumpkin seeds**
- **75g sunflower seeds**
- **1 teaspoon reduced-salt soy sauce**
- **¼ teaspoon chilli powder**

1 Preheat the oven to 190°C/375°F/gas mark 5.
2 Mix all the ingredients together and transfer to a baking tray.
3 Cook for 10 minutes until dried and lightly golden. Leave to cool then store in an airtight container, either in the fridge or the freezer.

PER SERVING: 72 kcals; 6g fat; 1g saturated fat; 2g carbohydrate; 0.02g sodium

tomato tofu cocktail

SERVES 2

- **1 x 410g tin chopped tomatoes**
- **100g silken tofu**
- **juice of ½ lime**
- **1 tablespoon Worcestershire sauce, or more to taste**
- **½ teaspoon hot pepper sauce**
- **4 ice cubes**
- **celery sticks, to serve**

1 Put the tinned tomatoes into a liquidiser goblet then add half a tin of cold water and the remaining ingredients.
2 Whizz until smooth then serve with the celery.

PER SERVING: 75 kcals; 3g fat; 0.3g saturated fat; 7g carbohydrate; 0.31g sodium

digestive biscuits

You can also bake these in bun tins to make a biscuity case for a dollop of fromage frais and fruit.

MAKES 14 BISCUITS

- **100g medium oatmeal**
- **100g brown bread flour with malted wheatgrain**
- **25g light muscovado sugar**
- **1 teaspoon baking powder**
- **2 tablespoons rapeseed oil**
- **4 tablespoons milk**

1 Preheat the oven to 190°C/375°F/gas mark 5.
2 Combine the dry ingredients in a bowl (or a food-processor) and mix in the oil and milk to make a firm dough. (If it feels a little too dry to roll out add a few drops of water.)
3 Roll the dough, as thinly as possible, between two layers of clingfilm. Stamp out 8–9cm rounds and transfer to a non-stick baking tray. Dampen and re-roll the trimmmings as necessary.
4 Bake for about 15 minutes until lightly golden. Leave to go cold on a wire rack then store in an airtight container.

PER SERVING: 75 kcals; 2g fat; 0.4g saturated fat; 12g carbohydrate; 0.05g sodium

mini seed snacks

These biscuits contain a great mix of seeds - the linseed, pumpkin and sesame seeds are a good plant source of omega 3 fatty acids and they will also provide beneficial phytoestrogens.

MAKES 30 (2 PER PORTION)

- 2 tablespoons pumpkin seeds
- 1 tablespoon sunflower seeds
- 1 tablespoon linseeds
- 1 tablespoon sesame seeds
- 200g brown bread flour with malted wheatgrain
- ½ teaspoon easy blend yeast
- ½ teaspoon yeast extract mixed with 1 teaspoon boiling water
- 2 tablespoons finely grated parmesan cheese

1 Preheat the oven to 200°C/400°F/gas mark 6. Lightly oil a 32 x 23cm baking tray.
2 Combine all the seeds in a bowl and mix well. Put the flour, yeast and half the seeds in a food-processor and mix to a firm dough with 150ml hand-hot water. Knead lightly then roll out thinly between two sheets of baking paper.
3 Lay the dough onto the baking tray and brush with the yeast extract. Press the remaining seeds on top and sprinkle with the cheese.
4 Bake for 10 minutes until lightly golden then carefully remove from the baking tray. Reduce the temperature to 160°C/325°F/gas mark 3. Cut the dough into 30 pieces and return to the oven for 15-20 minutes until fairly crisp and golden.
5 Leave to cool on a wire rack until completely cold and crisp. Store in an airtight container.

PER SERVING: 66 kcals; 2g fat; 0.4g saturated fat; 10g carbohydrate; 0.02g sodium

griddled courgettes
with lime and mint

Delicious warm or cold, this is more satisfying than a biscuit, but only 40 calories. They are also a great way to bump up your veg intake.

SERVES 4

- olive oil, for spraying/greasing
- 4 large courgettes
- 4 tablespoons chopped mint
- freshly ground black pepper
- 2 limes, halved

1 Preheat a non-stick ridged grill pan over high heat. When ready to cook spray it very lightly with olive oil.
2 Trim and cut each courgette lengthways into 8 slices. Lay the slices, in batches, on the grill pan and cook for 2-3 minutes each side until softened and marked with the ridges. Turn and cook on the other side.
3 Serve sprinkled with mint and pepper, and squeeze the lime halves over.

PER SERVING: 40 kcals; 1g fat; 0.2g saturated fat; 4g carbohydrate; 0g sodium

prune and hazelnut 'salami'

FOR WEIGHT MAINTENANCE

There's no meat in this fruity snack, but it is shaped like a salami. Toast the nuts in the oven at 190°C/375°F/gas mark 5 for about 15 minutes, or chop them first then toast them in a dry frying pan over medium heat. This 'salami' will keep in the fridge for up to 1 month.

SERVES 6

- **250g ready-to-eat prunes**
- **¼ teaspoon ground star anise**
- **1 teaspoon finely grated orange zest**
- **1 teaspoon sesame seeds**
- **25g shelled hazelnuts, toasted and chopped**

1 Roughly chop the prunes (you can do this in the food-processor) then mix well with the remaining ingredients.

2 Transfer to a piece of clingfilm and shape into a 'log', twisting the ends of the clingfilm tightly. Store in the fridge until required.

3 Cut a portion in slices as a quick snack straight from the fridge.

PER SERVING: 92 kcals; 3g fat; 0.3g saturated fat; 15g carbohydrate; 0.01g sodium

VARIATION For an Apricot and Pistachio variation, simply replace the prunes with dried apricots and the hazelnuts with pistachios.

PER SERVING: 98 kcals; 3g fat; 0.3g saturated fat; 16g carbohydrate; 0.01g sodium

soft cheese and orange dip

FOR WEIGHT MAINTENANCE

The citrus zest balances the richness of the cheese and dates in this unusual dip.

SERVES 4

- **40g stoned dates, chopped**
- **finely grated zest and juice of 1 orange**
- **100g light soft cheese**
- **2 dessert apples, cored and thinly sliced**

1 Put the dates and orange juice in a small saucepan and heat gently just until softened. Leave to go cold then beat in the zest and cheese.

2 Serve with the apple slices as dippers.

PER SERVING: 99 kcals; 3g fat; 2g saturated fat; 16g carbohydrate; 0.1g sodium

date and tahini dip

FOR WEIGHT MAINTENANCE

This is a Middle Eastern variation of the cheese and orange dip above.

SERVES 4

- **75g stoned dates, chopped**
- **finely grated zest and juice of 1 unwaxed lemon**
- **1 tablespoon tahini**
- **2 medium pears, quartered, cored and thinly sliced**

1 Put the dates in a small saucepan with the lemon juice and cook over a gentle heat just until the dates are softened, adding a dash of water if necessary. Cool, then stir in the lemon zest and tahini.

2 Serve with pear slices for dipping.

PER SERVING: 101 kcals; 2g fat; 0.3g saturated fat; 20g carbohydrate; 0.01g sodium

a pint of prawns
with herb dip

A classic recipe but with a lot less fat – I've used fat-free yogurt here instead of mayonnaise.

SERVES 2

- **250g cooked prawns in their shell, rinsed and dried**
- **1 x 150g tub 0% fat Greek yogurt**
- **1 garlic clove, crushed**
- **1 tablespoon chopped coriander**
- **2 teaspoons chopped mint**
- **¼ teaspoon freshly ground black pepper**

1 Pile the prawns into a tumbler and chill in the fridge until required.
2 Mix together the remaining ingredients, cover and ideally leave for at least 1 hour for the flavours to develop.
3 Serve the dip with the prawns, peeling them at the table.

PER SERVING: 86 kcals; 0.4g fat; 0.1g saturated fat; 4g carbohydrate; 0.33g sodium

dill and buttermilk rolls

Frozen rolls can be thawed and refreshed one at a time in the microwave. To prepare one of these from frozen, set it on a piece of kitchen paper and cook on high heat for 20–30 seconds only.

MAKES 18 ROLLS

- **500g brown bread flour with malted wheatgrain**
- **20g fresh dill, finely chopped**
- **1½ teaspoons bicarbonate of soda**
- **1 x 250g carton buttermilk**
- **about 150ml semi-skimmed milk**

1 Preheat the oven to 230°C/450°F/gas mark 8. Sprinkle a baking tray with flour.
2 In a large mixing bowl, stir together the flour, dill and bicarbonate of soda. Make a well in the centre and add the buttermilk and half the milk.
3 Mix to a soft yet not sticky dough, adding extra milk as necessary, then transfer to a lightly floured surface and shape into a ball.
4 Cut the dough into 18 equal pieces and roughly shape each one. Set on the prepared baking tray and bake for about 20 minutes until risen and crusty and hollow-sounding when tapped on the base.
5 Cool on a wire tray. Store in an airtight container. Freeze if preferred.

PER SERVING: 98 kcals; 1g fat; 0.2g saturated fat; 21g carbohydrate; 0.13g sodium

Indian-style cottage cheese

Scoop up this delicious dip with baby gem lettuce or chicory leaves.

SERVES 2

- **½ teaspoon cumin seeds**
- **50g red onion, finely chopped**
- **1 medium-sized red chilli, de-seeded and finely chopped**
- **2 tablespoons chopped coriander**
- **200g reduced-fat cottage cheese**

1 Dry-fry the cumin seeds in a small frying pan over a medium heat just until they smell fragrant.
2 Combine all the ingredients and mix well. Serve with salad leaves as suggested to scoop up the dip.

PER SERVING: 98 kcals; 2g fat; 0g saturated fat; 6g carbohydrate; 0.3g sodium

chilli bean pâté

Use chunks of raw vegetables as dippers – I like cucumber, celery or carrots.

SERVES 4

- **1 teaspoon olive oil**
- **1 shallot, finely chopped**
- **1 garlic clove, finely chopped**
- **1½ teaspoons ground cumin**
- **1½ teaspoons ground coriander**
- **½ teaspoon chilli powder**
- **1 x 410g tin kidney beans in water, drained and rinsed**
- **juice of ½ lime, or more to taste**

1 Heat the oil in a small frying pan and sauté the shallot and garlic until softened. Stir in the spices and cook, stirring over a gentle heat, for 30 seconds.
2 Put the beans, spice mixture and juice of ½ lime in a food-processor and pulse to a chunky texture, adding 1–2 tablespoons water, as required. Add extra lime juice to suit taste.
3 Serve with chunks of vegetables as suggested.

PER SERVING: 90 kcals; 2g fat; 0.1g saturated fat; 14g carbohydrate; 0.28g sodium

date and rhubarb sponge wedges

This sponge has a sweet and chewy texture. The dates and rhubarb keep it moist, so it will also freeze well (cut it into wedges first so that you can defrost a piece at a time).

SERVES 12
- 125g stoned dates, chopped
- 125g rhubarb, chopped
- 50g unsalted butter
- 125g brown bread flour with malted wheatgrain
- 2 teaspoons baking powder
- 2 medium eggs, beaten
- 1 teaspoon vanilla extract

1 Preheat the oven to 180°C/350°F/gas mark 4. Line the base of a 20cm sandwich tin with baking paper. Spray the sides very lightly with oil.

2 Put the dates in a small saucepan, add the rhubarb and 4 tablespoons cold water, then cover and simmer, stirring occasionally, until softened to a rough purée. Beat in the butter and allow to cool.

3 Put the flour in a mixing bowl, add the baking powder, date mixture, eggs and vanilla extract, and mix well.

4 Transfer to the prepared tin and level the surface. Bake for about 25 minutes until risen and just firm to the touch.

5 Cool on a wire rack. Store in an airtight container.

PER SERVING: 96 kcals; 5g fat; 3g saturated fat; 12g carbohydrate; 0.16g sodium

apricot beaker loaf

You don't even need scales for this one - all the measurements are based on a 300ml beaker. This loaf also freezes well.

MAKES 16 SLICES
- 90g (1 beaker) high-fibre bran cereal
- 50g (⅓ beaker) dark muscovado sugar
- 200g (1 beaker) ready-to-eat dried apricots, chopped
- 300ml (1 beaker) semi-skimmed milk
- 175g (1 beaker) brown bread flour with malted wheatgrain
- 1 tablespoon baking powder
- 1 tablespoon caraway seeds (optional)

1 Put the cereal in a bowl, mix in the sugar, apricots and milk, then cover and leave to soak for 2 hours or thereabouts.

2 Preheat the oven to 180°C/350°F/gas mark 4. Line a 900g loaf tin with baking paper.

3 Add the flour, baking powder and caraway seeds, if using, to the soaked cereal and beat well until evenly mixed. Transfer the mixture to the prepared tin and level the surface.

4 Bake for about 50 minutes until risen and firm to the touch. Cool in the tin then transfer to a wire rack until completely cold. Wrap in kitchen foil and store in an airtight container, or freeze in slices.

PER SERVING: 92 kcals; 1g fat; 0.3g saturated fat; 20g carbohydrate; 0.17g sodium

roasted soya beans

You can experiment with other seeds and herbs as you choose.

SERVES 8

- **200g soya beans**
- **4-6 sprigs of fresh rosemary**
- **1 teaspoon fennel seeds**
- **1 teaspoon cumin seeds**
- **freshly ground black pepper**

1 Soak the beans in cold water overnight. Drain and rinse. Transfer to a large saucepan and cover with boiling water. Bring back to the boil then simmer for 10 minutes. Drain thoroughly.
2 Preheat the oven to 200°C/400°F/gas mark 6. Line two baking trays with sheets of baking paper.
3 Divide the beans in half and pour onto the trays. Add the rosemary to one tray and the seeds to the other. Season both generously with pepper then mix well. Ensure the beans are in a single layer.
4 Roast for about 45-60 minutes, stirring occasionally, until crisp and golden. Switch off the oven and leave the beans to cool in the residual heat.
5 Discard the rosemary stalks – all the 'needles' will be crisp and will have fallen off. Store each tray of beans in a separate airtight container.

PER SERVING: 98 kcals; 5g fat; 0g saturated fat; 5g carbohydrate; 0g sodium

warm natural popcorn

It's best to cook this fresh as you want it. There's no need to add any oil to the pan. For 2 or 4 servings use a bigger pan and more popping corn.

SERVES 1

- **30g popping corn**
- **cinnamon or pepper for sprinkling, if liked**

1 Put the popping corn in a medium-sized saucepan over a medium-high heat. Cover with the lid and shake over the heat until you hear the corn start to 'pop'.
2 Reduce the heat to medium-low and leave the pan over the heat until all the popping stops. Don't be tempted to lift the lid before then! Sprinkle with cinnamon or pepper if liked, and serve at once.

PER SERVING: 88 kcals; 1g fat; 0.1g saturated fat; 19g carbohydrate; 0g sodium

red lentil bars with cucumber mint yogurt

A dish that can be made in advance and reheated for a quick nibble or a light lunch. You can also freeze any that you don't want immediately.

MAKES 24 BARS (12 PORTIONS)

- **1 tablespoon olive oil**
- **1 onion, finely chopped**
- **1 leek, finely chopped**
- **1 carrot, finely chopped**
- **1 teaspoon ground cumin**
- **1 teaspoon ground coriander**
- **¼ teaspoon dried chilli flakes**
- **175g dried red lentils**
- **400ml vegetable stock**
- **50g medium oatmeal**
- **1 egg, beaten**

FOR THE CUCUMBER MINT YOGURT

- **½ large cucumber, de-seeded and diced**
- **1 garlic clove, finely chopped**
- **12 mint leaves, chopped**
- **1 x 150g tub 0% fat Greek yogurt**

1 Preheat the oven to 190°C/375°F/gas mark 5. Line a 28 x 18cm baking tray with baking paper.

2 To make the cucumber mint yogurt, combine all the ingredients then cover and chill until required to allow the flavours to develop.

3 Heat the oil in a medium-sized saucepan and add the onion, leek and carrot and cook for 10 minutes over a low heat to soften but not colour the vegetables. Add the cumin, coriander and chilli and cook for a further 1 minute.

4 Add the lentils and stock and cook, uncovered, for about 20 minutes until the lentils are tender but not too mushy and the liquid has been absorbed. Cook for up to another 10 minutes if necessary to achieve this. Allow to cool a little then fold in the oatmeal and egg, and stir to combine.

5 Spread the mixture evenly into the prepared baking tray and bake for 30 minutes. Cut into bars and serve with the cucumber mint yogurt.

PER SERVING: 99 kcals; 3g fat; 0.4g saturated fat; 13g carbohydrate; 0.09g sodium

hot chocolate nightcap

This is a real treat for you to enjoy – warm, rich and perfect to send you to sleep. It is also much healthier than shop-bought products.

SERVES 1

- **1 tablespoon cocoa powder**
- **1 teaspoon golden caster sugar**
- **100ml semi-skimmed milk**

1 In a small saucepan, mix the cocoa powder and sugar with 6 tablespoons cold water. Place over a medium heat and stir until it comes to a simmer.
2 Whisk in the milk until heated through. If preferred, heat the milk separately and whisk until frothy then stir in the chocolate mixture. Serve at once.

PER SERVING: 99 kcals; 4g fat; 2g saturated fat; 13g carbohydrate; 0.06g sodium

banana loaf

So simple you can't really go wrong. The hint of spice brings a tasty warmth to this bread. Store in an airtight container or freeze in slices.

MAKES 16 SLICES

- **2 large bananas**
- **1 medium egg**
- **250g brown bread flour with malted wheatgrain**
- **1 tablespoon baking powder**
- **½ teaspoon ground nutmeg**
- **50g raisins or sultanas**
- **40g shelled pecan nuts, chopped**

1 Preheat the oven to 180°C/350°F/gas mark 4. Line a 900g loaf tin with baking paper.
2 Purée together the bananas, egg and 100ml cold water.
3 Mix the remaining ingredients together in a bowl and stir in the banana purée until evenly mixed.
4 Transfer to the prepared tin and bake for 35–40 minutes until risen and just firm to the touch. Cool slightly then remove from the tin and set on a wire rack until completely cold.

PER SERVING: 97 kcals; 3g fat; 0.3g saturated fat; 17g carbohydrate; 0.12g sodium

Most of the recipes in this chapter can be packed in Tupperware or flasks and reheated later - perfect for packed lunches.

portable food

a chunky potato soup

The chunks of bacon in this soup will give it a lovely smoky flavour and the carrots will provide some rich colour as well as lots of useful vitamins. You can freeze this soup.

SERVES 2

- **1 onion, roughly chopped**
- **2 garlic cloves, finely chopped**
- **2 rashers smoked streaky bacon, diced**
- **2 celery stalks, thinly sliced**
- **1 teaspoon fresh thyme leaves**
- **1 bay leaf**
- **2 medium carrots, sliced**
- **350g new potatoes, cut into 1cm pieces**
- **2 x 300ml tubs fresh chicken stock, made up to 1 litre with water**
- **3 tablespoons chopped flat-leaf parsley**
- **2 tablespoons 0% fat Greek yogurt**
- **freshly ground black pepper**

1 Put the onion, garlic and bacon in a medium-sized, non-stick saucepan and cook, covered, over a medium heat for about 8 minutes, stirring occasionally and adding a splash of water, as necessary.
2 Add the celery, thyme, bay leaf, carrots and potatoes and cook until the potatoes start to stick on the bottom of the pan – about 5 minutes.
3 Add the stock and bring to the boil. Simmer, covered, for about 15 minutes until the potatoes are tender and starting to fall apart.
4 Stir in the parsley and yogurt. Season to taste with black pepper.

PER SERVING: 292 kcals; 8g fat; 2g saturated fat; 42g carbohydrate; 0.93g sodium

a curried vegetable and lentil soup

Tamarind concentrate is available in supermarkets and Asian stores – follow instructions for diluting. The soup will keep in the fridge for up to 2 days, or freeze for up to 1 month.

SERVES 3

- **1 onion, chopped**
- **4 garlic cloves, chopped**
- **½ teaspoon red chilli flakes**
- **1 teaspoon freshly ground black pepper**
- **½ teaspoon ground cumin**
- **½ teaspoon ground coriander**
- **½ teaspoon turmeric**
- **1 ½ litres vegetable stock, made from 1 stock cube and water**
- **150g dried red lentils, washed**
- **200g butternut squash, cut in chunks**
- **2 carrots, sliced**
- **75g frozen sweetcorn kernels**
- **50g peas (fresh or frozen)**
- **4 spring onions, sliced**
- **1 green chilli, de-seeded and sliced**
- **1 tablespoon tamarind water**
- **1 tablespoon coriander leaves**
- **50g baby spinach leaves**
- **lime wedges, for squeezing (optional)**

1 In a liquidiser or food-processor, blend the onion, garlic, chilli flakes and spices with a little of the stock until you have an onion purée. Transfer to a large saucepan with the remaining vegetable stock and the lentils.
2 Bring to the boil, then reduce the heat, cover and simmer for 20 minutes. Add the butternut squash and carrots and cook for a further 15 minutes, then add the remaining ingredients and cook for a further 5 minutes. Serve with wedges of lime.

PER SERVING: 300 kcals; 3g fat; 0.3g saturated fat; 54g carbohydrate; 0.63g sodium

a type of panzanella salad

This quick, Italian-style bread salad will fill you up, and it's quick and easy to prepare.

SERVES 2

- 3 slices soya and linseed bread, cut into 2cm cubes
- 2 tablespoons sherry vinegar
- 4 tomatoes, cut into bite-sized chunks
- 4 spring onions, roughly chopped
- ½ cucumber, halved lengthways, de-seeded and cut in 1cm half moon shapes
- 1 x 320g jar whole sweet red peppers in brine, drained and well rinsed, each cut in four
- 1 red chilli, de-seeded and finely diced
- a handful of rocket, roughly chopped
- 6 basil leaves, shredded
- 3 teaspoons extra virgin olive oil
- freshly ground black pepper

1 Preheat the oven to 200ºC/400ºF/gas mark 6 then toast the bread cubes on a baking tray until golden (10–15 minutes), turning them from time to time. Transfer to a bowl.

2 Sprinkle the bread with the vinegar and set aside. Combine the remaining ingredients and season to taste. Fold in the bread cubes and leave for 15 minutes before serving to allow the flavours to develop.

PER SERVING: 277 kcals; 10g fat; 2g saturated fat; 38g carbohydrate; 0.69g sodium

chunky vegetable soup

We all know by now that we need to eat low GI foods, and this soup contains plenty. It will also freeze well for up to 1 month.

SERVES 6

- spray oil
- 1 onion, roughly chopped
- 2 garlic cloves, finely chopped
- 2 sage leaves, chopped
- 2 celery stalks, sliced
- 1 leek, sliced
- 2 carrots, sliced
- 175g small new potatoes, halved
- 1 x 410g tin chopped tomatoes
- 2 litres vegetable stock
- 1 courgette, sliced
- 125g peas (fresh or frozen)
- 125g green beans, cut in 3cm lengths
- 175g Savoy cabbage, finely shredded
- 50g baby spinach leaves
- 1 x 410g tin borlotti beans in water, drained and rinsed
- freshly ground black pepper
- 50g parmesan cheese, grated, to serve
- 6 slices soya and linseed bread, to serve

1 Put a large saucepan over a medium heat and spray with oil. Add the onion and garlic and cook for 5 minutes until the onion is softening. Add a splash of water as necessary.

2 Add the sage, celery, leek, carrots and potatoes and cook for 2 minutes, stirring from time to time. Add the tomatoes and stock and cook for 12–15 minutes until the potatoes are tender.

3 Add the remaining ingredients and cook for a further 5 minutes. Season to taste and serve with the grated parmesan and bread.

PER SERVING: 294 kcals; 8g fat; 2g saturated fat; 39g carbohydrate; 0.74g sodium

classic chicken mood soup

To accompany the soup, offer wedges of lime, thinly sliced red chillies and sprigs of basil.

SERVES 6

- 6 skinless chicken thighs
- 600ml fresh chicken stock
- 1 x 3cm piece of fresh ginger, washed and sliced
- 2 garlic cloves, bruised
- 2 tablespoons fish sauce (nam pla)
- 10 black peppercorns
- 2 onions, thinly sliced
- 125g sugarsnap peas, sliced
- 250g broccoli, cut in small pieces
- 6 spring onions, sliced
- 250g thin rice noodles
- 3 tablespoons chopped coriander

1 Put the chicken in a large saucepan or stockpot. Pour in the chicken stock and 1.8 litres water and add the ginger, garlic, fish sauce, peppercorns and onions. Bring just to the boil then reduce the heat and simmer, covered, for 20 minutes. Remove the chicken and allow to cool slightly then cut the meat into shreds or dice and discard the bones. Set aside until ready to use.
2 Continue to simmer the stock, uncovered, for a further 30 minutes or so to reduce by half. Strain the stock and return to the heat. Skim away any fat that is floating on the surface. Add the sugarsnaps, broccoli and spring onions and cook for 2 minutes.
3 Meanwhile cover the noodles with boiling water. Leave for 5 minutes, then drain.
4 Return the shredded chicken to the soup. Put the drained noodles into a soup tureen or six individual bowls and top with the chicken soup. Sprinkle with the coriander.

PER SERVING: 271 kcals; 3g fat; 1g saturated fat; 40g carbohydrate; 0.66g sodium

bunho beef with noodles

This is a classic Vietnamese dish. It has a base of fine rice noodles with a light stock and is topped with beef marinated in traditional flavours.

SERVES 4

- 1 garlic clove, crushed
- 1 medium onion, thinly sliced
- 1 x 5cm piece of lemongrass, tender inner part only, very finely chopped
- 1 red chilli, de-seeded and finely diced
- 1 teaspoon freshly ground black pepper
- 1 tablespoon fish sauce (nam pla)
- 2 teaspoons clear honey
- 200g fillet steak, thinly sliced
- 175g fine rice noodles
- 100g beansprouts
- 125g Chinese greens, finely shredded
- ½ cucumber, halved lengthways, de-seeded and grated
- 24 mint leaves, thinly sliced
- spray oil
- 1 x 300ml tub fresh beef stock, warmed
- 1 tablespoon natural roasted peanuts, chopped
- 1 teaspoon sesame seeds

1 In a large bowl, combine the garlic, onion, lemongrass, chilli, pepper, fish sauce and honey and marinate the beef in this mixture for 30 minutes.
2 Put the rice noodles in a saucepan or heatproof bowl, pour boiling water over them, cover and leave for 5 minutes then drain. Divide the noodles between individual deep bowls, then add the beansprouts, Chinese greens, cucumber and mint.
3 Heat a frying pan or griddle over a high heat and spray lightly with oil, if necessary. Sear the beef for 30 seconds each side then add to the bowls. Pour a little stock into each bowl, then sprinkle with the nuts and seeds.

PER SERVING: 295 kcals; 7g fat; 2g saturated fat; 44g carbohydrate; 0.47g sodium

smoked trout kedgeree

Race around the supermarket to buy yourself some hot-smoked trout – the remaining ingredients should be in your cupboard.

SERVES 4

- spray oil
- 1 onion, finely chopped
- 1 tablespoon curry paste
- 175g brown basmati rice, cooked
- 2 x 100g packs hot-smoked trout
- 3 tablespoons chopped parsley
- 1 tablespoon snipped chives
- 2 tablespoons 0% fat Greek yogurt
- lemon juice, to taste
- freshly ground black pepper
- 2 hard-boiled eggs, roughly chopped

1 Heat a non-stick frying pan then spray with oil and fry the onion over a medium heat for 8-10 minutes until softened without colouring, adding a splash of water as necessary.

2 Add the curry paste and 1 tablespoon water. Stir to combine then cook gently for a further 3 minutes. Add the rice and cook for a further 2 minutes, then flake in the trout and add the herbs and yogurt. Stir to combine and heat through gently to prevent the pieces of trout falling apart.

3 Season to taste with lemon juice and black pepper then fold in the hard-boiled eggs.

PER SERVING: 292 kcals; 9g fat; 2g saturated fat; 36g carbohydrate; 0.48g sodium

beetroot, potato and apple salad

Beetroot is a great root vegetable, but one that is woefully underused. Watch out for its juices as they can stain clothes and worksurfaces.

SERVES 3

- 400g new potatoes, washed
- 1 x 250g pack cooked beetroot in natural juice, diced
- 2 dessert apples, cored and thinly sliced
- 1 tablespoon raspberry vinegar
- 1 tablespoon olive oil
- freshly ground black pepper
- 50g alfalfa sprouts
- 1 x 250g tub cottage cheese
- 1 tablespoon chopped chives

1 Steam or cook the potatoes in boiling water for 15-20 minutes until tender. Drain and when cool enough to handle, cut into bite-size pieces.

2 Mix with the beetroot and apples then whisk the vinegar, oil and pepper together and toss with the salad.

3 Stir in the alfalfa sprouts, cottage cheese and chives just before serving.

PER SERVING: 291 kcals; 8g fat; 3g saturated fat; 42g carbohydrate; 0.36g sodium

crab cakes with cucumber relish

A delicious light meal that is popular with adults and children, served hot or cold.

SERVES 4

FOR THE CRAB CAKES

- **450g cooked white crab meat**
- **4 spring onions, thinly sliced**
- **1 teaspoon grated fresh ginger**
- **1 red chilli, de-seeded and finely chopped**
- **½ red pepper, de-seeded and finely diced**
- **2 tablespoons finely chopped coriander**
- **200g frozen sweetcorn kernels, defrosted and well drained**
- **2 tablespoons 0% fat Greek yogurt**
- **1 egg yolk**
- **8 tablespoons seeded breadcrumbs* see below right**
- **spray oil**

FOR THE CUCUMBER RELISH

- **2 cucumbers, halved lengthways and de-seeded**
- **1 tablespoon golden caster sugar**
- **4 tablespoons rice vinegar**
- **1 hot red chilli, de-seeded and finely diced**
- **2 shallots, finely diced**
- **4 tablespoons chopped coriander leaves**
- **25g natural roasted peanuts, chopped**
- **2 teaspoons fish sauce (nam pla)**

1 Combine all the crab cake ingredients except the breadcrumbs and spray oil and pulse in a food-processor just until the mixture can be pressed together to form 12 cakes. Lightly coat with the breadcrumbs, cover and chill for up to 12 hours.

2 To make the cucumber relish, cut the cucumber in 5mm slices. Dissolve the sugar in the vinegar, and toss the cucumber slices in this. Stir in the chilli, shallots and coriander. Just before serving, sprinkle with the peanuts and add the fish sauce.

3 To cook the crab cakes, spray a light coating of oil in a large non-stick frying pan over a medium heat and add the crab cakes. Do not overcrowd, cook in batches if required. Cook for 2-3 minutes on each side until golden and heated through. Serve with the cucumber relish.

* To make the breadcrumbs, dry 2-3 slices soya and linseed bread in a preheated oven at 190ºC/375ºF/gas mark 5 for about 25 minutes until crisp and brittle. Allow to cool on a wire rack, then blitz in a food-processor until the crumbs are fine but retain some texture.

PER SERVING: 304 kcals; 9g fat; 2g saturated fat; 25g carbohydrate; 0.9g sodium

poached baby veg with asparagus and lemon sauce

Every so often I really enjoy a good bowl of vegetables with a very light lemon sauce.
See what you think of this.

SERVES 4

- **50g faro (spelt) or wholewheat berries, soaked in cold water overnight**
- **600ml vegetable stock**
- **12 baby carrots**
- **8 baby turnips**
- **12 small new potatoes**
- **12 button onions**
- **16 asparagus spears**
- **12 button Brussels sprouts**
- **75g extra fine green beans**
- **100g peas (fresh or frozen)**
- **125g tiny broccoli florets**
- **8 cherry tomatoes**

FOR THE SAUCE

- **2 egg yolks**
- **juice of 1-2 lemons**
- **2 teaspoons cornflour**
- **2 tablespoons 0% fat Greek yogurt**
- **freshly ground white pepper**

1 Drain and cook the faro in boiling water for about 15 minutes until tender. Drain the faro and keep warm. Meanwhile, in a large saucepan, bring the vegetable stock to the boil and add the baby carrots, turnips, potatoes and onions, all left whole. Cook for 12-15 minutes until thoroughly cooked. Remove and set aside to keep warm.

2 Cut the tops off the asparagus spears and reserve, and cook the rest of the stalks in the vegetable stock until tender. Remove and set aside to be used for the sauce.

3 Cook the button sprouts in the stock for 3 minutes then add the beans and cook for a further 2 minutes, then add the peas, broccoli and reserved asparagus spears, and cook for 3 minutes more. Remove all the green vegetables and combine them with the root vegetables in a bowl.

4 Boil the vegetable stock until only 300ml remains. Plunge the cherry tomatoes into the stock and cook for 30 seconds. Remove and add to the other vegetables.

5 To make the sauce, purée the asparagus stalks in a food-processor with the egg yolks, the juice of 1 lemon and the cornflour, adding a little of the reserved vegetable stock as necessary. Pass the mixture through a sieve into a small saucepan. Set over a low heat, then gradually add the hot vegetable stock, whisking constantly until the sauce is lightly thickened but has not boiled. Remove from the heat and whisk in the Greek yogurt. Season to taste with the white pepper and extra lemon juice, as wished.

6 Divide the faro and vegetables between four warm bowls and drizzle with the sauce.

PER SERVING: 289 kcals; 7g fat; 1g saturated fat; 44g carbohydrate; 0.23g sodium

Indonesian king prawn curry

This is one of my favourite curries although it is not Indian by origin – it is much less rich and calorific than a 'real' curry would be, but it packs a punch of vibrant flavours. This dish also won the curry challenge on my tv show, *Saturday Cooks*. If you make more than you need, you can always save the leftovers for the next night or put in the freezer.

SERVES 2

FOR THE PRAWNS
- **1 teaspoon lemon juice**
- **1 teaspoon turmeric**
- **½ teaspoon chilli powder**
- **200g peeled large raw prawns, deveined**

FOR THE CURRY
- **spray rapeseed oil**
- **2 medium onions, each cut in 12 wedges**
- **4 garlic cloves, sliced**
- **3cm piece of fresh ginger, peeled and grated**
- **3 green chillies, de-seeded and sliced**
- **1 green pepper, de-seeded and cut in 2-3cm pieces**
- **1 teaspoon ground coriander**
- **1 teaspoon ground cumin**
- **4 tomatoes, cut into chunks**
- **1 tablespoon tamarind paste mixed with 3 tablespoons water**
- **a handful of coriander leaves, roughly chopped**
- **sliced spring onions, to garnish**
- **50g brown basmati rice, cooked, to serve**

1 Combine the lemon juice, turmeric and chilli powder with 1 tablespoon water, then massage this mixture into the prawns and leave to marinate for 20 minutes.

2 Meanwhile, to make the curry base heat a non-stick wok or frying pan then spray with oil. Add the onions and cook for 6-8 minutes until the onions are translucent but not brown, adding a splash of water as necessary.

3 Add the garlic, ginger and chillies and cook for a further 2 minutes then add the green pepper and spices and stir-fry for 3 minutes. Add the tomatoes and tamarind water, increase the heat and cook for 3 minutes, adding a little water as necessary.

4 Heat a small non-stick frying pan and spray with oil. Cook the prawns with their marinade and a splash of water, if necessary, for 2-3 minutes until they turn pink. Fold into the curry sauce and serve at once, sprinkled with coriander and spring onions. Serve with the rice alongside.

PER SERVING: 299 kcals; 5g fat; 0.6g saturated fat; 43g carbohydrate; 0.28g sodium

spicy bean jacket potato

A quick low GI chunky dip or filling. Serve with a green salad.

SERVES 4

- 4 x 250g baking potatoes
- 1 x 410g tin red kidney beans in water or borlotti beans in water, drained and rinsed
- 1 x 150g tub 0% fat Greek yogurt
- 2 tomatoes, de-seeded and diced
- 1 red chilli, de-seeded and finely diced
- 1 garlic clove, crushed
- 2 tablespoons chopped coriander
- 1 teaspoon ground cumin
- 1 teaspoon ground coriander
- ½ small red onion, finely diced
- juice of ½-1 lime
- freshly ground black pepper
- green salad, to serve

1 Preheat the oven to 200°C/400°F/gas mark 6. Scrub the potatoes and prick with a fork. Bake for 50-60 minutes until cooked through.
2 Mash half the beans and fold into the yogurt. Add the remaining ingredients and the whole beans and stir well. Season to taste with pepper and use to fill the split potatoes.

PER SERVING: 298 kcals; 2g fat; 0.1g saturated fat; 60g carbohydrate; 0.05g sodium

chicken and salmon miso soup

Surf and Turf (combining seafood and meat) works well with grills, so why not with this main course soup?

SERVES 4

- 2 teaspoons miso paste
- 2 teaspoons oyster sauce
- 2 teaspoons reduced-salt soy sauce
- 1 tablespoon grated ginger
- 1 teaspoon crushed garlic
- finely grated zest and juice of 1 orange
- 1 litre fresh chicken stock
- 200g chicken breast, thinly sliced
- 175g skinless salmon fillet, cut in 1cm pieces
- 2 heads bok choi, finely shredded
- 100g dried thin wheat noodles, cooked according to packet instructions
- 4 spring onions, thinly sliced
- freshly ground white pepper

1 In a large saucepan, combine the miso paste, oyster sauce, soy sauce, ginger and garlic and the orange zest and juice. Stir in the stock and bring to a simmer.
2 Add the chicken, salmon and bok choi. Simmer for 3-4 minutes then add the noodles and spring onions. Season to taste with white pepper.

PER SERVING: 300 kcals; 9g fat; 1g saturated fat; 26g carbohydrate; 0.96g sodium

cauliflower rarebit

This is a quick and filling lunch or dinner best served straight from the grill rather than packed and reheated later.

SERVES 6

- **600g cauliflower florets (1 large cauliflower)**
- **75g reduced-fat red leicester cheese, grated**
- **1 tablespoon Dijon mustard**
- **2 medium eggs, beaten**
- **2 teaspoons Worcestershire sauce**
- **4 tablespoons 0% fat Greek yogurt**
- **pinch of grated nutmeg**
- **freshly ground black pepper**
- **6 slices soya and linseed bread, toasted**
- **250g baby spinach leaves, wilted**
- **2 x 410g tins borlotti beans in water, drained, rinsed and warmed**
- **12 tomatoes, cut in half and grilled**

1 Preheat the grill to very hot. Steam or cook the cauliflower in boiling water for about 5 minutes until just tender but retaining some firmness. Drain and keep warm.

2 Meanwhile beat together the cheese, mustard, eggs, Worcestershire sauce and yogurt with a little nutmeg and black pepper.

3 Place the toast on a baking tray, top with the spinach and beans then arrange the cauliflower on top. Divide the cheese mixture between the cauliflower toasts, coating the cauliflower evenly. Flash under the grill until the cheese is bubbling and golden. Serve at once with the grilled tomatoes.

PER SERVING: 330 kcals; 9g fat; 2g saturated fat; 39g carbohydrate; 0.74g sodium

avocado dip
with pitta crisps

This is a great little recipe for a quick snack. The pitta crisps can be stored in an airtight container for 4-5 days.

SERVES 3

- **3 pitta breads**
- **a handful of flat-leaf parsley leaves**
- **a handful of baby spinach leaves**
- **1 garlic clove, crushed**
- **finely grated zest and juice of ½ unwaxed lemon**
- **dash of Worcestershire sauce**
- **dash of Tabasco**
- **½ teaspoon ground cumin**
- **½ teaspoon ground coriander**
- **1 large avocado, peeled and stoned**
- **4 tablespoons 0% fat Greek yogurt**
- **¼ teaspoon freshly ground black pepper**
- **3 tomatoes, cut in wedges, to serve**

1 Preheat the oven to 170°C/325°F/gas mark 3. Slit the pitta in two then cut each half into 6 triangles and arrange on a baking tray. Cook in the oven for 15-20 minutes until lightly golden and very crispy. Leave to cool on a wire rack.

2 Meanwhile, bring a pan of water to the boil and plunge in the parsley and spinach. Cook for 2 minutes then drain and plunge into iced water. Drain, squeeze dry and roughly chop.

3 Put the spinach mixture in a food-processor with the remaining ingredients except the tomatoes. Pulse until fairly smooth then check the seasoning. Serve with the tomato wedges and pitta crisps.

PER SERVING: 357 kcals; 16g fat; 2g saturated fat; 45g carbohydrate; 0.38g sodium

mini low gi bread and tomato pizza

Prepare the ingredients at home and then whip this up for lunch, so long as you have access to an oven. Instead of using pizza base or puff pastry, use a low GI bread - 'pizza' in a flash!

SERVES 4

- 1 x 410g tin cannellini beans in water, drained and rinsed
- 2 tablespoons black olive paste
- 50g pine nuts, toasted
- 3 spring onions, finely sliced
- 4 slices soya and linseed bread (or other seeded bread), toasted on one side
- 4 tomatoes, sliced
- 1 teaspoon fennel seeds
- ¼ teaspoon chilli powder
- 1 tablespoon clear honey
- 3 teaspoons extra virgin olive oil
- rocket leaves, to serve

1 Preheat the oven to 200ºC/400ºF/gas mark 6. Mash half the beans with the back of a fork. Fold in the remaining beans, the olive paste, pine nuts and spring onions.

2 Spread the untoasted sides of the seeded bread with the bean paste and arrange the sliced tomato on top.

3 Combine the spices with the honey and olive oil and drizzle over the tomatoes. Place the bread pizzas on a baking tray and cook in the oven for 12-15 minutes until the tomatoes have slightly collapsed. Serve piping hot, with the rocket leaves.

PER SERVING: 353 kcals; 19g fat; 2g saturated fat; 35g carbohydrate; 0.4g sodium

mixed grain, seed and herb salad

We know we should eat them, but how do you make grains and seeds a little more exciting? With the addition of herbs, salad vegetables, and even fruit as here, they can be very flavoursome and enjoyable. This salad will keep in the fridge in an airtight container for up to 48 hours.

SERVES 4

- 75g wild rice
- 100g bulgur wheat
- 25g linseeds
- 25g hemp seeds
- 25g pumpkin seeds
- 50g flat-leaf parsley, roughly chopped
- 3 tablespoons roughly chopped mint
- 3 tablespoons roughly chopped coriander
- 6 spring onions, thinly sliced
- 2 plum tomatoes, chopped
- 75g raisins
- 75g ready-to-eat dried apricots, chopped
- finely grated zest and juice of 1 unwaxed lemon
- 1 teaspoon freshly ground black pepper

1 Cook the wild rice according to packet instructions. Drain well. Meanwhile, soak the bulgur in 600ml boiling water for 15 minutes, then drain and squeeze dry.

2 When cool, combine the rice with the bulgur and seeds, then stir in the herbs, spring onions, tomatoes, dried fruit and lemon zest.

3 Just before serving add the lemon juice and pepper. Toss thoroughly to combine.

PER SERVING: 345 kcals; 8g fat; 1g saturated fat; 61g carbohydrate; 0.04g sodium

kippers with apples and horseradish

For breakfast or lunch. A quick dish to put together, but one with lots of taste and texture.

SERVES 4

- **4 kipper fillets**
- **6 tablespoons 0% fat Greek yogurt**
- **1 tablespoon lemon juice**
- **1 teaspoon grated horseradish**
- **1 teaspoon cider vinegar**
- **3 dessert apples, cored and diced**
- **4 spring onions, finely sliced**
- **freshly ground black pepper**
- **16 crispbreads, to serve**

1 Place the kipper fillets in a shallow container, cover with boiling water and leave for 5-7 minutes, then drain thoroughly. Discard the skin then break the fillets up by shredding the flesh with two forks. Remove as many bones as possible.

2 Put the yogurt in a bowl, then stir in the lemon juice, horseradish, vinegar, apples and spring onions.

3 Fold the fish flakes into this mixture. Season to taste with plenty of black pepper and extra horseradish, if wished. Serve with crispbreads.

PER SERVING: 328 kcals; 11g fat; 2g saturated fat; 44g carbohydrate; 0.59g sodium

bean and salad wrap

A versatile quick lunch: eat it warm or cold for something a little different from your average office sandwich.

SERVES 4

- **spray rapeseed oil**
- **3 spring onions, thinly sliced**
- **3 garlic cloves, crushed**
- **1 red chilli, de-seeded and finely chopped**
- **1 teaspoon ground cumin**
- **1 teaspoon ground coriander**
- **1 x 200g tin chopped tomatoes**
- **1 x 410g tin borlotti beans in water, drained and rinsed**
- **2 tablespoons chopped coriander**
- **4 flour tortillas, warmed**
- **1 medium avocado, peeled and sliced**
- **75g iceberg lettuce, shredded**
- **2 tablespoons 0% fat Greek yogurt**

1 Heat a non-stick frying pan, spray on some oil, add the spring onions, garlic and chilli and cook for 2 minutes over a medium heat, adding a splash of water if necessary. Add the spices and cook for a further 1 minute then add the tomatoes and beans. Simmer until the liquid has reduced to a thick sauce consistency. Stir in the coriander.

2 Lay the tortillas out on the counter and spread with some bean mixture, top with avocado and lettuce and drizzle with the yogurt. Roll the tortillas up, tucking in the ends. Slice in half and eat warm, or leave to cool then wrap in greaseproof paper or clingfilm for transporting.

PER SERVING: 284 kcals; 11g fat; 1g saturated fat; 38g carbohydrate; 0.65g sodium

asian chicken and lettuce rolls

This satisfying light lunch is perfect for casual eating. Each person spoons a little mince into the lettuce leaves, rolls them up if wished and bites into the contrast of the crisp, cool leaves and the warm filling.

SERVES 4

- **400g chicken mince**
- **1 red chilli, de-seeded and finely diced**
- **2 spring onions, finely chopped**
- **1 garlic clove, crushed**
- **1 teaspoon grated ginger**
- **1 teaspoon sesame oil**
- **25g water chestnuts or beansprouts, chopped**
- **2 tablespoons chopped coriander**
- **2 tablespoons chopped cashew nuts**
- **1 carrot, finely diced**
- **2 tablespoons oyster sauce**
- **2 teaspoons clear honey**
- **16-20 romaine or cos lettuce leaves**
- **200g brown basmati rice, cooked, to serve**
- **lime wedges, to serve**

1 Mix the chicken mince with the chilli, spring onions, garlic, ginger and sesame oil. Heat a large non-stick frying pan over a medium heat and cook the mince mixture for about 5 minutes, breaking the meat up with the back of a fork until golden brown.
2 Add the water chestnuts, coriander, cashews, carrot, oyster sauce and honey, stir to combine and continue to heat until the chicken is cooked through.
3 Serve the mince with the lettuce leaves, cooked rice and lime wedges to squeeze.

PER SERVING: 343 kcals; 7g fat; 1g saturated fat; 45g carbohydrate; 0.49g sodium

more than a mouthful tomato soup

This main course soup has loads of texture and flavour – perfect one-pot dining. Freeze any leftovers in portion-size containers and keep for up to 1 month.

SERVES 4

- **1 large onion, finely diced**
- **2 garlic cloves, finely chopped**
- **1 tablespoon tomato purée**
- **1 dried hot red chilli, left whole**
- **2 x 410g tin chopped tomatoes**
- **2 bay leaves**
- **2 teaspoons ground cumin**
- **1 teaspoon sugar**
- **150g chorizo sausage, skinned and diced**
- **1 x 410g tin cannellini beans in water, drained and rinsed**
- **100g brown basmati rice, rinsed**
- **3 tablespoons chopped parsley**
- **freshly ground black pepper**

1 Put all the ingredients except for the parsley and pepper in a large saucepan. Add 1.3 litres water, or enough to give you the consistency you prefer and bring to a simmer. Cover and simmer gently for 30 minutes.
2 Remove the chilli and bay leaves, then add the parsley and season to taste. Serve piping hot.

PER SERVING: 326 kcals; 11g fat; 4g saturated fat; 42g carbohydrate; 0.43g sodium

main
meals

Here are great
meal ideas for
all occasions
– a sunday roast,
quick chicken
curry or
veggie pasta.
Make sure you
serve them with
vegetables and
sufficient starchy
carbohydrates
for your needs.

tomato and wheat bake

SERVES 4

- 3 teaspoons olive oil
- 1 onion, finely chopped
- 2 garlic cloves, finely chopped
- 1 red pepper, de-seeded and cut into 1cm dice
- 1 teaspoon each thyme leaves and dried oregano
- 1 x 410g tin chopped tomatoes
- 12 basil leaves, ripped
- 1 teaspoon each ground allspice and dried chilli
- 600ml vegetable stock
- 250g bulgur wheat
- 1 x 150g tub 0% fat Greek yogurt
- 4 medium eggs, beaten
- 2 tablespoons snipped chives
- 3 tomatoes, sliced
- 400g green beans, steamed, to serve

1 Heat the oil in a large saucepan then add the onion, garlic and red pepper and cook gently for 8-10 minutes, adding a splash of water as necessary. Stir in the thyme and oregano and cook for a further 5 minutes, adding more water as required. Stir in the tomatoes and cook for 10 minutes, uncovered, before adding the basil, allspice and chilli.

2 Add the stock to the sauce and bring to the boil. Stir in the bulgur, reduce the heat and cook for 10-15 minutes, until the bulgur is tender, stirring regularly. The liquid should be all but absorbed.

3 Turn off the heat and allow to stand covered for 10 minutes. If the mixture is too wet, uncover and cook over a low heat until it becomes thicker. Season to taste with pepper and allow to cool.

4 Meanwhile preheat the oven to 180°C/350°F/ gas mark 4, then whisk the yogurt into the eggs and season with pepper and chives. Place the bulgur in a shallow baking dish, top with the sliced tomatoes then pour over the egg mixture. Bake in the oven for 30-35 minutes until golden.

PER SERVING: 334 kcals; 6g fat; 0.6g saturated fat; 61g carbohydrate; 0.39g sodium

a quick vegetable stir-fry

A vegetarian dish that meat-eaters will also find delicious and that provides a good balance of proteins and carbohydrate.

SERVES 2

- spray oil
- 250g firm tofu, cut into 3cm pieces
- 2 garlic cloves, crushed
- 1 x 3cm piece of fresh ginger, peeled and grated
- 1 tablespoon hot chilli sauce
- 250g butternut squash, cut in 1cm dice
- 2 tablespoons reduced-salt soy sauce
- 1 teaspoon clear honey
- 175g button mushrooms, halved
- 4 spring onions, sliced
- 2 heads bok choi, roughly chopped
- a handful of coriander leaves
- 100g brown basmati rice, cooked, to serve

1 Heat a large non-stick frying pan over a high heat then spray with oil. Cook the tofu pieces in batches until golden on all sides, remove and set aside.

2 To the same pan, add the garlic, ginger, chilli sauce and butternut squash with 150ml water and cook until the butternut is starting to soften, about 5 minutes. Add extra water, as necessary.

3 Stir in the soy sauce, honey and mushrooms and cook for 3 minutes.

4 Add the spring onions and bok choi and return the tofu to the pan. Cook until the tofu has heated through and the bok choi has wilted, about 2 minutes. Finally fold in the coriander leaves and serve immediately with the freshly cooked rice.

PER SERVING: 282 kcals; 7g fat; 1g saturated fat; 39g carbohydrate; 0.9g sodium

wild mushroom
and barley 'risotto'

I like ceps and girolles but if you can't find them, use field mushrooms, oyster or shiitake, or a combination. Serve with a green salad.

SERVES 4

- **3 teaspoons olive oil**
- **1 onion, finely chopped**
- **2 garlic cloves, finely chopped**
- **1 teaspoon soft thyme leaves**
- **1 bay leaf**
- **350g assorted mushrooms, wiped and sliced**
- **250g pearl barley, rinsed**
- **75ml red wine**
- **750–900ml vegetable stock, heated**
- **175g frozen peas, defrosted**
- **100g baby spinach leaves**
- **3 tablespoons chopped parsley**
- **freshly ground black pepper**

1 Heat the oil in a large pan over a medium heat. Add the onion, garlic, thyme and bay leaf and cook gently, stirring occasionally for 8-10 minutes. Add a splash of water as necessary.

2 Stir in the mushrooms and cook for 4-5 minutes, again adding a splash of water as necessary. Add the pearl barley and stir. Pour in the wine and boil to evaporate.

3 Add a ladleful of stock and simmer, uncovered, until it has been absorbed. Repeat the process until 750ml stock has been absorbed - about 30 minutes - and the barley is tender.

4 Stir in the peas, spinach and parsley and simmer for 5 minutes, adding the extra stock if you want a soft risotto consistency. Season to taste with pepper.

PER SERVING: 353 kcals; 6g fat; 1g saturated fat; 64g carbohydrate; 0.44g sodium

FOR WEIGHT MAINTENANCE

penne with
artichokes and
salad leaf pesto

A store-cupboard pasta dish - all you need to buy is some feta and a bag of salad.

SERVES 4

- **300g dried penne, or other pasta shape**
- **50g rocket leaves**
- **25g baby spinach leaves**
- **1 tablespoon flaked almonds, toasted**
- **2 garlic cloves, chopped**
- **½ teaspoon dried red chilli flakes**
- **finely grated zest and juice of 1 unwaxed lemon**
- **1 tablespoon capers, rinsed and drained**
- **2 tablespoons finely grated parmesan cheese**
- **1 x 290g jar wood-roasted artichokes, drained, well rinsed and each one halved**
- **freshly ground black pepper**
- **50g feta cheese, crumbled**

1 Cook the pasta according to the packet instructions.

2 Meanwhile, in a food-processor, pulse together half the rocket, all the spinach, almonds, garlic, chilli flakes, lemon zest and juice, capers and parmesan, then transfer to a bowl.

3 Drain the pasta, retaining 100ml cooking water. Add the water to the pesto, then add the pesto and artichokes to the pasta, toss to combine and return to a very gentle heat to warm through.

4 Stir in the reserved rocket and season with pepper. Transfer to warm bowls and top with the crumbled feta. Serve immediately.

PER SERVING: 444 kcals; 18g fat; 4g saturated fat; 60g carbohydrate; 0.7g sodium

spaghetti with courgettes, ricotta, basil and lemon

Keep the courgettes al dente, and try using spelt spaghetti for a change.

SERVES 4

- **300g dried spaghetti**
- **1 tablespoon olive oil**
- **2 garlic cloves, finely chopped**
- **2 courgettes, thinly sliced**
- **finely grated zest and juice of 1 unwaxed lemon**
- **50g ricotta cheese, crumbled**
- **1 tablespoon grated parmesan cheese**
- **2 tomatoes, diced**
- **8 basil leaves, ripped**
- **1 tablespoon pine nuts, toasted**
- **freshly ground black pepper**

1 Cook the pasta in boiling water for 1 minute less than the recommendation on the packet. Drain, reserving a little of the cooking water.

2 Meanwhile, heat the olive oil in a large frying pan or wok and fry the garlic and courgettes over a medium heat, turning regularly, for about 3 minutes until just starting to colour.

3 Add the pasta to the courgettes together with 3-4 tablespoons cooking water. Stir in the lemon zest and juice, both cheeses, the tomatoes, basil and pine nuts and toss to combine. Season with pepper and serve immediately.

PER SERVING: 349 kcals; 8g fat; 2g saturated fat; 59g carbohydrate; 0.04g sodium

hot prawns, cold salad

The taste sensations in this salad work well together, as does the contrast between hot and cold.

SERVES 2

FOR THE PRAWNS

- **1 garlic clove, crushed**
- **2cm piece of fresh ginger, peeled and grated**
- **2 tablespoons chopped coriander**
- **1 tablespoon chopped mint**
- **¼ teaspoon dried chilli flakes**
- **2 teaspoons liquid honey**
- **250g shelled raw prawns, ideally with tails intact, rinsed**
- **60g brown basmati rice, cooked**

FOR THE SALAD

- **½ cucumber, sliced lengthways, de-seeded and cut in 5mm half moons**
- **1 small red onion, halved and thinly sliced**
- **16 cherry tomatoes, halved**
- **1 tablespoon sunflower seeds**
- **1 red chilli, de-seeded and thinly sliced**
- **3 tablespoons coriander leaves**
- **1 tablespoon chopped mint leaves**
- **1 tablespoon ripped basil leaves**
- **1 teaspoon fish sauce (nam pla)**
- **juice of 1 lime**
- **½ teaspoon golden caster sugar**

1 Pulse together in a mini food-processor the garlic, ginger, coriander, mint, chilli flakes and honey to form a smooth paste. Alternatively, very finely chop the garlic, ginger and herbs then stir in the chilli flakes and honey. Toss the prawns in this paste, cover and leave to marinate in the fridge for at least 30 minutes or up to 12 hours.

2 Meanwhile prepare the salad. In a large bowl, combine the cucumber, onion, tomatoes, sunflower seeds, chilli and herbs, and set aside. Mix together the fish sauce, lime juice and sugar and stir until the sugar has dissolved. Set aside.

3 Preheat a steamer. Place the prawns in a dish in the steamer, cover and cook over a high heat for 4 minutes. You will most probably have to do this in two batches.

4 Just before serving, pour the dressing over the salad and toss to combine. Divide between two plates and serve with the hot prawns. Serve the rice separately.

PER SERVING: 296 kcals; 5g fat; 0.7g saturated fat; 37g carbohydrate; 0.51g sodium

spiced cod on a bed of chorizo-infused beans

You may need extra carbs with this meal.

SERVES 4

- **50g cooking chorizo, skinned and diced**
- **1 onion, chopped**
- **1 garlic clove, crushed**
- **1 teaspoon oregano leaves, roughly chopped**
- **250g podded or frozen baby broad beans (or 125g frozen soya beans)**
- **500g new potatoes, cut into 5mm slices**
- **½ teaspoon each ground cumin and coriander**
- **1 teaspoon paprika**
- **½ teaspoon turmeric**
- **2 teaspoons clear honey**
- **lemon juice**
- **4 x 125g cod fillets with skin**
- **spray olive oil**

1 Put the chorizo in a hot non-stick pan and cook over a medium heat until it releases its red oils. Add the onion, garlic and oregano leaves and cook for 5-7 minutes until the onion has softened, adding a splash of water, as necessary.

2 Add the beans and potatoes with 250ml water. Cover with a circle of wet greaseproof paper and a lid and cook over a very low heat for 30-40 minutes. Do not allow to dry out, top up with water as needed.

3 Meanwhile preheat the oven to 220ºC/425ºF/ gas mark 7. Combine the spices with the honey and sufficent lemon juice to make a thin paste. Use to coat the flesh side of the cod.

4 Spray a non-stick ovenproof frying pan with olive oil. Over a high heat cook the cod, skin side down, for 5 minutes, then place in the oven for 10 minutes until golden and very lightly caramelised.

5 Divide the bean mixture between four warm plates then top with the cod.

PER SERVING: 290 kcals; 5g fat; 1g saturated fat; 31g carbohydrate; 0.16g sodium

greengrocer's casserole

Oats aren't just for breakfast, here they help thicken this vegetarian stew.

SERVES 4

- **3 teaspoons olive oil**
- **1 onion, finely chopped**
- **2 large leeks, cut in 2cm rings, then well washed**
- **3 garlic cloves, crushed**
- **1 fennel bulb, chopped**
- **75g porridge oats**
- **1.2 litres vegetable stock**
- **1 medium potato, cut in 2cm cubes**
- **1 x 410g tin chopped tomatoes**
- **2 large courgettes, cut in 2cm pieces**
- **½ butternut squash, peeled and cut in 2cm dice**
- **½ Savoy cabbage, roughly chopped**
- **a few sprigs of thyme**
- **2 bay leaves**
- **150g spinach leaves, washed and large stalks removed**
- **½ teaspoon grated nutmeg**
- **pinch of ground allspice**
- **freshly ground black pepper**

1 Heat the olive oil in a flameproof casserole dish and add the onion, leeks, garlic and fennel and cook gently for 8-10 minutes until the vegetables have softened. Add a splash of water, as necessary.

2 Stir in the oats and cook over a slightly higher heat until the oats have turned lightly golden, stirring regularly. Remove from the heat.

3 Meanwhile heat the stock to boiling in a large saucepan then add the potato and the tomatoes and simmer for 10 minutes. Add the courgettes, squash and cabbage with the thyme and bay leaves. Simmer for another 10 minutes.

4 Fold in the spinach, spices and oat mixture. Cook for 10 minutes until thick. Season to taste.

PER SERVING: 332 kcals; 9g fat; 1g saturated fat; 47g carbohydrate; 0.76g sodium

steak with beans and greens

SERVES 4

- **75g dried small pasta shapes**
- **1 teaspoon olive oil**
- **1 onion, thinly sliced**
- **large pinch of chilli flakes**
- **1 garlic clove, crushed**
- **1 x 410g tin white beans (such as haricot, cannellini or butter) in water, drained and rinsed**
- **100g baby spinach leaves**
- **4 tablespoons chopped parsley**
- **350g lean rump, sirloin or fillet steak, cut thickly**
- **freshly ground black pepper**

FOR THE VINAIGRETTE

- **finely grated zest and juice of 1 unwaxed lemon**
- **1 tablespoon Dijon mustard**
- **1 shallot, finely chopped**
- **2 tablespoons baby capers, rinsed**
- **1 teaspoon chopped anchovies or anchovy paste**
- **¼ teaspoon freshly ground black pepper**

1 First make the vinaigrette by combining all the ingredients with 2 tablespoons iced water and set aside.

2 Cook the pasta. Heat the olive oil in a saucepan then add the onion, chilli flakes and garlic and cook over a medium heat for 6-8 minutes until softened but not browned. Add a splash of water, as necessary.

3 Stir in the beans and cook until warm, then fold in the spinach and parsley and cook until wilted. Stir in the pasta and half the vinaigrette.

4 Meanwhile season the steak with pepper and cook on a preheated griddle pan until charred on both sides and cooked to your liking. Allow the meat to rest for 5 minutes then slice thinly.

5 Divide the beans, then top with steak and drizzle with the remaining vinaigrette and any meat juices.

PER SERVING: 304 kcals; 6g fat; 2g saturated fat; 35g carbohydrate; 0.43g sodium

oriental chicken salad

A crunchy oriental salad that is light to eat and easy to prepare.

SERVES 2

- **1 medium chicken breast, cooked and finely shredded**
- **1 large shallot, thinly sliced**
- **100g beansprouts, rinsed**
- **150g Chinese cabbage, finely shredded**
- **1 large carrot, very thinly sliced**
- **½ cucumber, halved lengthways, de-seeded and cut in 5mm slices**
- **100g cherry tomatoes, halved**
- **8 radishes, sliced**
- **2 tablespoons coriander leaves**
- **1 tablespoon shredded mint leaves**
- **20g unsalted roasted peanuts, chopped**
- **50g rice noodles, prepared according to packet instructions and well drained**

FOR THE DRESSING

- **4 tablespoons lime juice**
- **1 tablespoon fish sauce (nam pla)**
- **2 bird's-eye chillies, de-seeded and finely chopped**
- **2 garlic cloves, crushed**
- **2 teaspoons clear honey**

1 Combine all the dressing ingredients in a small bowl or jug and leave to sit for 30 minutes to allow the flavours to develop.

2 Combine all the salad ingredients apart from the noodles in a large bowl.

3 Just before serving, toss the dressing through the salad until well mixed.

4 Spoon the noodles into 2 large bowls and top with salad.

PER SERVING: 337 kcals; 9g fat; 2g saturated fat; 39g carbohydrate; 0.66g sodium

white bean and lamb stew

A great winter-warming dish, easy to prepare and very satisfying. Freeze any leftovers.

SERVES 4

- **spray olive oil**
- **300g very lean lamb (from the leg or neck fillet), cut into small pieces**
- **1 onion, roughly chopped**
- **2 celery stalks, cut into 2cm chunks**
- **2 carrots, peeled and cut into 2cm chunks**
- **2 garlic cloves, sliced**
- **2 sprigs of rosemary**
- **1 tablespoon Worcestershire sauce**
- **1 x 410g tin chopped tomatoes**
- **2 bay leaves**
- **2 x 410g tins black-eye beans in water, drained and rinsed**
- **300g Savoy cabbage, roughly chopped**
- **freshly ground black pepper**

1 Preheat the oven to 180°C/350°F/gas mark 4.
2 Heat a flameproof casserole dish over a high heat then spray lightly with oil and fry the lamb in batches until browned all over. Set aside.
3 To the same casserole dish, add the onion, celery, carrots, garlic and rosemary and cook, adding a splash of water, until the vegetables have started to soften – 8-10 minutes.
4 Return the lamb to the casserole and add the Worcestershire sauce, tomatoes and bay leaves. Stir to combine then add 300ml water. Cover and cook in the oven for 45 minutes, then stir in the beans and cabbage, adding extra water as necessary. Return to the oven for a further 15 minutes. Season with pepper to taste.

PER SERVING: 316 kcals; 8g fat; 2g saturated fat; 35g carbohydrate; 0.21g sodium

an andalucian pork stew

If you're not a fan of black pudding, use an extra 100g of pork fillet instead. If you make more than you need, you can freeze half.

SERVES 4

- **spray olive oil**
- **200g pork fillet cut into 3cm pieces**
- **1 onion, roughly chopped**
- **2 celery stalks, chopped**
- **2 carrots, thinly sliced**
- **3 garlic cloves, finely chopped**
- **125g green beans, topped and tailed**
- **500ml chicken stock**
- **1 x 410g tin chickpeas in water, drained and rinsed**
- **1 x 410g tin cannellini beans in water, drained and rinsed**
- **100g black pudding, diced**
- **2 red peppers, charred and peeled, de-seeded and cut into strips, or use tinned or from a jar, well rinsed**
- **freshly ground black pepper**

1 Heat a large non-stick pan over a high heat and spray with oil. Add the pork to the pan and brown all over. Remove and set aside. Add the onion, celery and carrots to the pan and cook gently, adding a splash of water as necessary until they start to soften. Stir in the garlic, green beans and the stock and simmer for 8-10 minutes.
2 Return the browned meat to the pan. Add the chickpeas and cannellini beans and bring to a simmer. Cover and cook over a low heat for 2-3 minutes.
3 Meanwhile dry-fry the black pudding in a small non-stick frying pan. Add the black pudding and peppers to the stew and cook for a further 5 minutes. Season with pepper to taste.

PER SERVING: 350 kcals; 11g fat; 1g saturated fat; 38g carbohydrate; 0.8g sodium

paprika tuna with green and white pea mash

Simple, yet tasty and very quick to make.

SERVES 4

- ½ teaspoon olive oil
- 1 teaspoon sweet paprika
- 1 teaspoon coarsely ground black pepper
- 4 thick tuna fillets, about 100g each
- spray oil
- 100g watercress, well washed and with large stalks removed
- lemon juice or red wine vinegar, to sprinkle
- 500g new potatoes, boiled in their skins, to serve

FOR THE MASH

- 150ml chicken stock
- 250g frozen peas
- 2 x 410g tins chickpeas in water, drained and rinsed
- squeeze of lemon juice

1 Preheat the oven to 220ºC/425ºF/gas mark 7.
2 Mix the olive oil with the paprika and pepper and coat the tuna with it. Lightly spray an oven tray with oil and place the tuna on this. Bake for 4-5 minutes for medium rare or 7-8 minutes for more well cooked.
3 Meanwhile make the mash. Bring the stock to the boil in a saucepan. Add the frozen peas and boil for 2 minutes. Stir in the chickpeas and cook until they are heated through and most of the stock has evaporated. Remove from the heat, roughly mash with a potato masher, and season to taste with lemon juice and pepper.
4 Sprinkle the tuna with the lemon juice or red wine vinegar and serve on a bed of pea mash with the watercress and boiled potatoes on the side.

PER SERVING: 399 kcals; 8g fat; 1g saturated fat; 47g carbohydrate; 0.21g sodium

herby mackerel

SERVES 4

- 4 small mackerel (about 180g each)
- 1 slice soya and linseed bread
- 1 tablespoon each chopped parsley and coriander
- finely grated zest of 1 unwaxed lemon and 1 orange
- ½ teaspoon each ground cumin and ground coriander
- pinch of chilli flakes
- ½ teaspoon olive oil
- 100ml fish or chicken stock
- 600g new potatoes, cooked

FOR THE TOMATO SALAD

- 6-8 medium-sized tomatoes, sliced
- ½ medium red onion, very thinly sliced
- 1 tablespoon each chopped parsley and coriander
- 2 teaspoons orange or lemon juice
- freshly ground black pepper

1 Preheat the oven to 200ºC/400ºF/gas mark 6.
2 Remove the heads from the mackerel then split along the belly and remove the guts. Wash thoroughly and pat dry with kitchen paper. Open out each fish so that it lies skin-side up and press firmly along the length to loosen the backbone. Carefully lift the bone from the flesh then cut off at the tail end leaving the tail intact. Rinse and dry.
3 In a food-processor, pulse the bread with the herbs, zests, spices, chilli flakes and olive oil until it makes fine crumbs.
4 Arrange the mackerel flesh-side up in a large baking dish and sprinkle with the breadcrumbs. Pour the stock around the mackerel but not over.
5 Cook in the oven for 8-10 minutes until the fish is opaque.
6 Meanwhile, combine all the salad ingredients. Serve the mackerel with any juices from the baking dish and the salad and potatoes.

PER SERVING: 430 kcals; 22g fat; 4g saturated fat; 33g carbohydrate; 0.23g sodium

herb and nut-crusted sole

Dover or lemon, the choice is yours, but I think lemon sole represents excellent value and this topping gives the fish another dimension.

SERVES 4

- **1 tablespoon snipped chives**
- **2 tablespoons chopped flat-leaf parsley**
- **1 teaspoon rosemary leaves**
- **1 slice day-old seeded bread, crusts removed**
- **juice of ½ lemon**
- **15g toasted hazelnuts or flaked almonds, chopped**
- **2 teaspoons plain flour, for dusting**
- **paprika**
- **freshly ground black pepper**
- **4 x 100g fillets of lemon or Dover sole, skin on**
- **1 egg, beaten**
- **spray olive oil**
- **lemon wedges, to serve**

FOR THE VEGETABLES

- **350g new potatoes, cut in wedges and cooked**
- **spray olive oil**
- **½ teaspoon finely chopped rosemary leaves**
- **paprika**
- **freshly ground black pepper**
- **250g baby broad beans, fresh or frozen, and skinned if preferred**
- **125g peas, fresh or frozen**

1 Put the chives, parsley, rosemary, bread and lemon juice in a food-processor and blend to fine green crumbs. Stir in the nuts and set aside.

2 For the vegetables, preheat the oven to 200ºC/400ºF/gas mark 6. Place the potatoes in a non-stick roasting tin and spray with a light coating of olive oil. Season with rosemary, paprika and ground black pepper. Cook for about 20 minutes, turning from time to time, until lightly crisp. Meanwhile, boil the broad beans and peas – 3 minutes for frozen or up to 10 minutes for fresh. Drain and toss with the potatoes and keep warm.

3 For the fish: season the flour with paprika and black pepper and dust the flesh side of the fish. Put the beaten egg in a shallow plate and the nut crumb mixture in another. Dip the flesh side of each fillet first in the egg, and then the crumbs, pressing gently to ensure an even coating.

4 Heat a large ovenproof frying pan, ideally non-stick, and spray with a light mist of olive oil. Place the fish in the pan skin-side down and cook for 3 minutes. Turn them and transfer to the oven, and cook for 6 minutes.

5 Divide the vegetables between four warm plates then top with the sole. Serve with lemon wedges to squeeze.

PER SERVING: 297 kcals; 8g fat; 2g saturated fat; 29g carbohydrate; 0.19g sodium

FOR WEIGHT MAINTENANCE **trout** in a pea and artichoke stew

You can now buy fillets from large trout that look very similar to salmon, but are cheaper.

SERVES 4

- **1 x 260g jar wood-roasted artichokes, drained and rinsed**
- **finely grated zest and juice of 1 unwaxed lemon**
- **450ml vegetable stock**
- **1 tablespoon chopped thyme**
- **750g new potatoes, diced**
- **400g frozen peas**
- **400g trout fillet, cut in 2cm cubes**
- **4 tablespoons chopped parsley**
- **freshly ground black pepper**

1 Put the artichokes, lemon zest and juice, stock, thyme and potatoes in a wide, shallow flameproof casserole, and cook, covered, over a medium heat for about 25 minutes until the potatoes are tender. Add a little water, as necessary.

2 Add the peas and trout and cook gently for a further 5-7 minutes until the fish is just opaque. Sprinkle with parsley and season to taste with pepper. Serve in warm bowls.

PER SERVING: 445 kcals; 18g fat; 3g saturated fat; 42g carbohydrate; 0.67g sodium

spiced mussels
with tomatoes

Mussels are very good value. Scrub the shells well to remove any grit and pull off the 'beards'. Rinse thoroughly, discarding any with broken shells or that do not close when tapped.

SERVES 2

- **1 teaspoon olive oil**
- **1 onion, finely diced**
- **2 garlic cloves, crushed**
- **½ teaspoon chilli flakes**
- **1 teaspoon ground cumin**
- **1 teaspoon ground coriander**
- **½ teaspoon turmeric**
- **100ml dry white wine**
- **1 x 410g tin chopped tomatoes**
- **1 kg mussels, thoroughly cleaned**
- **2 tablespoons chopped parsley**
- **finely grated zest of 1 unwaxed lemon**
- **2 slices oat, soya and linseed bread (see page 49), to serve**

1 Heat the olive oil in a deep saucepan, add the onion and cook over a medium heat for 6 minutes until translucent. Add half the garlic, all the chilli and spices and cook for a further 2 minutes, stirring regularly. Add the white wine and heat through for 3-4 minutes then add the tomatoes and bring to the boil.

2 Add the mussels and cook, covered with a lid, over a high heat for 4-6 minutes, shaking the pan from time to time until the shells open.

3 Transfer the mussels to four warm bowls, discarding any that have not opened, then stir the remaining garlic, the parsley and lemon zest into the sauce. Cook for 1 minute then pour over the mussels. Serve with the seeded bread.

PER SERVING: 335 kcals; 8g fat; 1g saturated fat; 36g carbohydrate; 0.72g sodium

baked sardines with tomato

SERVES 4

- 8 medium sardines, filleted (400g filleted weight)
- 4 small tomatoes
- freshly ground black pepper
- finely grated zest of ½ unwaxed lemon
- 65g reduced-fat mozzarella, drained and diced
- 1 teaspoon fresh thyme leaves
- 100g baby spinach leaves, to serve

FOR THE SWEET POTATOES

- 2 sweet potatoes peeled and cut in chunks
- juice of ½ lemon
- 1 teaspoon fresh thyme leaves
- ½ teaspoon freshly ground black pepper

1 Preheat the oven to 220ºC/425ºF/gas mark 7. Toss the sweet potatoes with the flavouring ingredients and transfer to a non-stick roasting tin. Bake for 40 minutes, turning occasionally, until tender.

2 Prepare the sardines: discard the heads and guts and wash thoroughly, removing any black membrane from inside the gut cavity. Turn the fish skin-side up and press along the backbone from head to tail to loosen. Remove the back bone. Rinse thoroughly and dry on kitchen paper.

3 Dice the tomatoes and set them in a sieve over a small bowl to collect all the juices. Arrange the sardines flesh-side up on a non-stick baking tray and season with pepper.

4 Mix the well-drained tomatoes with the lemon zest, diced mozzarella and thyme and pile onto the fish fillets. Cook in the oven for 10 minutes.

5 Add the reserved tomato juice to the sweet potatoes and return to the oven while the fish cooks. Serve the sardines and sweet potatoes at once with a handful of fresh spinach leaves.

PER SERVING: 339 kcals; 12g fat; 3g saturated fat; 34g carbohydrate; 0.23g sodium

tuna, pink grapefruit and avocado salad

FOR WEIGHT MAINTENANCE

A lovely refreshing salad that is light yet full of healthy goodness.

SERVES 2

- 1 pink grapefruit
- 1 small avocado, peeled, stoned and diced
- 1 x 410g tin cannellini beans in water, drained and rinsed
- 1 x 200g tin tuna in spring water, drained and flaked
- 50g baby spinach leaves
- 2 slices oat, soya and linseed bread (see page 49), to serve

FOR THE DRESSING

- 1 tablespoon raspberry vinegar
- ½ medium red onion, finely diced
- 1 teaspoon clear honey
- 2 teaspoons fish sauce (nam pla)
- 1 tablespoon chopped coriander
- 1 teaspoon chopped mint

1 Using a small serrated knife, peel the grapefruit, discarding all the white pith. Cut between the membranes of the grapefruit to extract the segments. Do this over a bowl to catch the juices then squeeze the grapefruit trimmings after you have taken all the segments out. You should end up with about 4 tablespoons juice. Reserve the juice and put the segments in a bowl.

2 Add the avocado, beans and tuna to the grapefruit and toss to combine.

3 Add the dressing ingredients to the grapefruit juice and whisk to combine, then pour over the grapefruit salad. Add the spinach leaves and toss lightly. Serve at once with the bread.

PER SERVING: 441 kcals; 14g fat; 2g saturated fat; 49g carbohydrate; 0.6g sodium

poached salmon and tahini sauce
with aubergine salad

Poaching keeps the salmon wonderfully moist. A microwave, if you have one, is a good way to cook the aubergine - prick it and cook at high heat for 5 minutes then chop once it's cooled slightly.

SERVES 4

- 2 onions, sliced
- 4 x 125g salmon fillets
- 100g bulgur wheat, cooked according to packet instructions

FOR THE TAHINI SAUCE

- 1 x 150g tub 0% fat Greek yogurt
- 1 tablespoon tahini
- 1 garlic clove, crushed
- lemon juice, to taste
- 1/2 teaspoon freshly ground black pepper

FOR THE AUBERGINE SALAD

- 25g walnut pieces
- 1 tablespoon sesame seeds
- 1 medium aubergine, cut into 2cm chunks
- 1 tomato, diced
- 1 small red onion, finely diced
- a small handful of flat-leaf parsley leaves, finely shredded
- a small handful of coriander leaves, finely shredded
- a small handful of fenugreek leaves (optional)
- 1 garlic clove, crushed
- 1/2 teaspoon sumac (optional)
- juice of 1 lemon
- freshly ground black pepper

1 For the aubergine salad, preheat the oven to 180°C/350°F/gas mark 4. Spread the walnuts and sesame seeds onto a baking tray and cook for 8-10 minutes, shaking them around from time to time so they colour evenly. Once cool, roughly chop.

2 Steam the aubergine cubes for 10 minutes or until tender. Tip into a colander and leave to cool then squeeze gently to extract some of their water. Just before serving, combine with the rest of the salad ingredients.

3 For the salmon, pour 750ml water into a wide, shallow saucepan and add the sliced onions. Bring to a simmer then poach the salmon fillets, covered, for 10 minutes. Carefully lift the salmon out of its poaching liquor and transfer to kitchen paper to drain. Allow to cool slightly then peel off the skin and gently scrape away the dark flesh on the underside, if preferred.

4 Meanwhile, prepare the tahini sauce by whisking all the ingredients together until smooth.

5 Serve the salmon at room temperature with the bulgur wheat, salad and tahini sauce.

PER SERVING: 446 kcals; 21g fat; 4g saturated fat; 30g carbohydrate; 0.09g sodium

quick chicken curry

This is a delicious light curry, perfect for a week-night supper. If you make more than you need, you could freeze and reheat the curry – but don't freeze the rice.

SERVES 4

- 1 tablespoon rapeseed oil
- 1 onion, sliced
- 1 teaspoon finely chopped garlic
- 1 teaspoon grated ginger
- 2 green chillies, de-seeded and finely chopped
- 2 large courgettes, halved lengthways then sliced
- 1 teaspoon turmeric
- 3 tomatoes, each cut into 8 pieces
- 150g frozen peas
- 400g cooked chicken, cut in bite-size pieces
- 100g baby spinach leaves
- 4 tablespoons chopped coriander
- 1 tablespoon garam masala
- 150g brown basmati rice, cooked

1 Heat the oil in a large, wide, non-stick saucepan or wok. Add the onion and cook, covered, over a medium heat until softened but not browned, 8-10 minutes. Stir in the garlic, ginger and chillies and cook for a further 1 minute.

2 Add the courgettes and turmeric, pour in 4 tablespoons water then cover and cook over a gentle heat for 10-12 minutes until the courgettes have softened. Stir from time to time.

3 Add the tomatoes and stir to combine. Cover and cook for 4-5 minutes until the tomatoes have softened.

4 Stir in the peas, chicken, spinach, coriander and garam masala with another 4-6 tablespoons water. Cook for about 5 minutes until the chicken is heated through and the spinach has wilted. Serve with the freshly cooked basmati rice.

PER SERVING: 427 kcals; 13g fat; 3g saturated fat; 44g carbohydrate; 0.13g sodium

FOR WEIGHT
MAINTENANCE

grilled chicken with stir-fried spinach and lentils

A good, healthy way to end the day, this isn't just any old grilled chicken,
but one packed with flavour.

SERVES 4

- ½ teaspoon ground cumin
- ½ teaspoon ground coriander
- ½ teaspoon freshly ground black pepper
- 4 x 125g chicken breast fillets, skinless
- spray olive oil

FOR THE MANGO YOGURT

- 1 medium mango cut in 1cm dice
- 1 red chilli, de-seeded and finely diced
- ½ tablespoon chopped mint
- 1 tablespoon mango chutney
- 1 teaspoon curry paste
- 1 x 150g tub 0% fat Greek yogurt

FOR THE SPINACH

- 175g red lentils
- 1 tablespoon rapeseed oil
- 3 garlic cloves, bruised
- 1 dried chilli
- 500g baby spinach leaves, washed
- 1 tablespoon reduced-salt soy sauce
- freshly ground black pepper
- 25g roasted natural peanuts, chopped

1 First make the mango yogurt: combine the mango, chilli and mint, and set aside. Mix the chutney and curry paste together then fold in the yogurt. Combine the yogurt with the mango and set aside for at least 30 minutes for the flavours to infuse.

2 When ready to cook the chicken, preheat the grill to high. Combine the three spices and dust the chicken breasts with the mixture. Spray the chicken lightly with oil and cook under the preheated grill for 7–8 minutes on each side, turning once. Set aside to keep warm.

3 Meanwhile, cook the lentils in boiling water for 7–8 minutes until tender yet still with a little 'bite'. Drain thoroughly. Heat a large wok until very hot then add the oil, garlic and chilli and cook until the garlic is deep golden and the chilli has turned dark brown. Discard the garlic and chilli from the oil, add the spinach a little at a time over a high heat until wilted. Stir in the lentils then add the soy sauce and pepper to taste.

4 Pile the spinach mixture onto four warm plates. Slice the chicken (it looks like more that way!) and arrange it over the spinach, sprinkle with the peanuts and serve with the mango yogurt.

PER SERVING: 443 kcals; 10g fat; 2g saturated fat; 40g carbohydrate; 0.53g sodium

sausages with white beans and roasted peppers

A great way of getting more from a few sausages. Be sure to choose good-quality sausages with a high meat content.

SERVES 2

- 4 extra lean pork sausages, cut in 2-3cm chunks
- spray oil
- 4 garlic cloves, finely chopped
- 1 onion, roughly chopped
- 1 x 320g jar whole sweet red peppers in brine, drained, rinsed and roughly chopped
- 1 x 410g tin cannellini beans in water, drained and rinsed
- 150g baby spinach leaves
- 4 tablespoons chopped flat-leaf parsley
- finely grated zest and juice of ½ unwaxed lemon
- freshly ground black pepper

1 Preheat the grill to high and cook the sausage pieces until brown all over, remove and set aside.
2 Heat a large non-stick pan over a medium heat and spray with oil. Add half the garlic and all the onion to the pan and cook gently, adding a splash of water as necessary, until the onion is translucent, about 8 minutes.
3 Add the peppers, beans and 4 tablespoons water and cook for 5 minutes. Add the sausages and spinach and cook for a further 5 minutes.
4 Meanwhile, in a mini food-processor or pestle and mortar, blend together the remaining garlic, the parsley and lemon zest and juice. Add this to the pan and stir well. Season with pepper to taste and serve immediately.

PER SERVING: 393 kcals; 9g fat; 2g saturated fat; 47g carbohydrate; 0.86g sodium

rice noodles with chicken, prawns and squid

This is a really quick and easy stir-fry that also contains lots of green veg.

SERVES 4

- 250g rice noodles
- spray rapeseed oil
- 4 garlic cloves, crushed
- 2 red chillies, de-seeded and finely diced
- 1 skinless chicken breast fillet, finely shredded
- 1 medium egg, beaten
- 1 tablespoon reduced-salt soy sauce
- 1 tablespoon oyster sauce
- 100g sugarsnap peas, coarsely shredded
- 100g Savoy cabbage, finely shredded
- 50g beansprouts
- 180g prepared squid, cut in 2cm strips
- 8 shelled raw prawns
- 4 spring onions, sliced in 1cm batons
- a small handful of coriander leaves

1 Put the noodles in a pan or heatproof bowl, pour boiling water over them and soak for 1-2 minutes until softened. Drain and rinse under cold water, and set aside.
2 Heat a non-stick wok or frying pan until very hot then spray with oil. Add the garlic and chilli and stir-fry for 30 seconds. Add the chicken and noodles and toss to combine. Stir-fry for 2 minutes.
3 Pour in the beaten egg and toss to combine.
4 Add the soy sauce, oyster sauce, sugarsnaps and cabbage and stir for 2 minutes.
5 Add the beansprouts, squid and prawns and cook for a further 3-4 minutes, just until the prawns are pink. Serve immediately, garnished with spring onions and coriander leaves.

PER SERVING: 325 kcals; 4g fat; 0.7g saturated fat; 47g carbohydrate; 0.46g sodium

paillard of venison
on spring greens with blackberry sauce

Here the venison steaks are beaten thin to tenderise them – it also means that they will cook faster. The easiest way to beat the meat is to put it between two pieces of clingfilm then, using a rolling pin or wooden mallet, beat it firmly, working from the centre of the meat outwards to flatten it.

SERVES 4

- **250g blackberries**
- **3 tablespoons cider vinegar**
- **300ml fresh beef stock**
- **1 tablespoon olive or rapeseed oil**
- **4 spring onions, chopped**
- **500g spring greens, finely shredded**
- **25g flaked almonds, toasted**
- **4 x 125g venison steaks (either from loin or haunch), beaten thin**
- **freshly ground black pepper**
- **1 tablespoon redcurrant jelly**
- **snipped chives, to garnish (optional)**
- **400g new potatoes, cooked and drained, to serve**

1 In a liquidiser, purée half the blackberries with the cider vinegar and all but 4 tablespoons of the stock until smooth, then pass through a fine sieve to remove the pips.

2 Pour the blackberry purée into a saucepan and cook over a medium heat until reduced to 200ml – about 15 minutes. Set aside.

3 Heat half the oil in a large saucepan, add the spring onions and cook for 1 minute. Add the reserved 4 tablespoons stock and the spring greens and stir to combine. Cover and cook over a medium heat for 7 minutes until the greens have wilted. Fold in the toasted almonds.

4 Meanwhile, heat the remaining oil in a large non-stick frying pan. Season the venison generously with pepper and cook the paillards over a high heat for 1½ minutes each side. Cook them in two batches if necessary. Set aside but keep warm.

5 Add the redcurrant jelly to the venison pan with a couple of spoonfuls of blackberry sauce, scraping up any bits and bobs stuck to the bottom of the pan. Add the remaining blackberry sauce with the reserved blackberries and cook until the jelly has melted. Check the seasoning.

6 Spoon the greens onto four warm plates and surround with the blackberries and their sauce. Top the greens with the venison and sprinkle with chives, if wished. Serve with warm new potatoes.

PER SERVING: 400 kcals; 13g fat; 1g saturated fat; 35g carbohydrate; 0.27g sodium

sunday pot roast

This reduced-calorie pot roast is sure to become a favourite in your household. Chantenay carrots are small and sweet, and now available in most supermarkets.

SERVES 6

- **1kg piece boneless and skinless pork loin, excess fat removed**
- **2 teaspoons dried sage**
- **freshly ground black pepper**
- **2 large onions, each cut in 6 pieces**
- **500g sweet potatoes, cut in chunks**
- **500g chantenay carrots, scrubbed, or large carrots, cut in chunks**
- **300ml unsweetened apple juice**
- **2 dessert apples, cored and each cut into 6 wedges**
- **400g fine green beans, cooked**

1 Preheat the oven to 190°C/375°F/gas mark 5. Wipe the meat then sprinkle the surface of the fat with half the sage and season with pepper. Set it in an ovenproof casserole dish, cover and cook for 30 minutes.

2 Add the onions, sweet potatoes, carrots, apple juice and the rest of the sage and return to the oven for 45 minutes until the vegetables are almost tender.

3 Add the apple wedges and return to the oven for a further 15 minutes. Test the meat with a skewer to make sure that it is cooked, then remove from the oven and leave to rest for about 15 minutes before carving.

4 Serve with the green beans.

PER SERVING: 339 kcals; 7g fat; 2g saturated fat; 41g carbohydrate; 0.11g sodium

baked turkey and vegetable pilaff

SERVES 4

- **spray oil**
- **1 onion and 1 garlic clove, both finely chopped**
- **1 teaspoon soft thyme leaves**
- **2 bay leaves**
- **1 teaspoon ground coriander**
- **1 teaspoon ground cumin**
- **1 teaspoon turmeric**
- **1/2 teaspoon chilli powder**
- **250g turkey fillet, cut in strips**
- **2 leeks, sliced**
- **2 large carrots, sliced**
- **250g butternut squash, cut into 3cm chunks**
- **175g brown basmati rice, rinsed**
- **500ml chicken stock**
- **100g frozen peas**
- **3 tomatoes, diced**
- **4 tablespoons chopped coriander or parsley**
- **freshly ground black pepper**

1 Preheat the oven to 180°C/350°F/gas mark 4. Set a flameproof casserole dish over a medium heat and spray with oil. Add the onion and garlic and cook gently for 5 minutes, adding a splash of water as necessary. Add the thyme, bay leaves and spices. Stir then add the turkey and toss to coat with the spice mixture. Cook for 2 minutes.

2 Add the leeks, carrots and butternut squash and cook for 3 minutes, then add the rice, stock, peas and tomatoes. Bring to the boil, cover and cook in the oven for 30-40 minutes until the rice is tender and most of the liquid has been absorbed.

3 Remove from the oven and fluff up the rice. Cover with the lid again and leave for 3-5 minutes. Fold in the herbs, season with pepper and serve.

PER SERVING: 350 kcals; 5g fat; 0.7g saturated fat; 54g carbohydrate; 0.4g sodium

spicy vegetable curry

Many people think that curries are difficult to make, but that's not necessarily the case as most of them use only five main spices which you can keep in your store-cupboard at all times. Like most curries, this will freeze well - but don't freeze the rice.

SERVES 4

- **3 teaspoons rapeseed oil**
- **2 onions, each cut in 8 wedges through the root**
- **4 garlic cloves, crushed**
- **1 teaspoon ground cumin**
- **2 teaspoons ground coriander**
- **1 teaspoon turmeric**
- **½ teaspoon chilli powder**
- **1 teaspoon garam masala**
- **1 teaspoon freshly ground black pepper**
- **100g green or brown lentils, rinsed**
- **1 medium sweet potato cut in 2.5cm chunks**
- **1 medium aubergine, cut in 1cm chunks**
- **100g button mushrooms, wiped**
- **3 tomatoes, cut in wedges**
- **50g baby spinach leaves**
- **1 x 150g tub 0% fat Greek yogurt**
- **1 tablespoon coriander leaves**
- **200g brown basmati rice, cooked**

1 Heat the oil in a large saucepan, add the onions and garlic and cook over a medium heat for 8-10 minutes until softened and without too much colour.

2 Add the spices and cook until they smell aromatic - about 2 minutes. Add the lentils and stir to combine then add the sweet potato and aubergine and cook for 5 minutes. Pour in 600ml water, bring to a simmer then cook, covered, for a further 15 minutes.

3 Add the mushrooms and cook for 8 minutes, then stir in the tomatoes and spinach. Cook for 5 minutes, adding extra water as necessary to give a thick sauce consistency.

4 Fold in the yogurt and coriander. Serve with the freshly cooked rice.

PER SERVING: 410 kcals; 6g fat; 1g saturated fat; 76g carbohydrate; 0.18g sodium

Asian calf's liver with vegetables

Asian flavours work so well with liver. This recipe is particularly good with calf's liver, but lamb's liver or chicken liver are good substitutes.

SERVES 4

- **400g calf's liver cut in 2cm strips**
- **4 spring onions, very finely chopped**
- **1 garlic clove, crushed**
- **¼ teaspoon dried chilli flakes**
- **1 teaspoon sesame oil**
- **2 tablespoons reduced-salt soy sauce**
- **2 teaspoons clear honey**
- **1 tablespoon cornflour**
- **1 tablespoon rapeseed oil**
- **2 carrots, thinly sliced**
- **250g button mushrooms, quartered**
- **200g sugarsnap peas, trimmed**
- **3cm piece of fresh ginger, peeled and finely shredded**
- **100g brown basmati rice, cooked**
- **coriander leaves, to garnish**

1 Put the liver in a large bowl, then add a quarter of the spring onions, the garlic, chilli flakes, sesame oil, soy sauce, honey and cornflour and toss to combine. Cover and leave to marinate for at least 1 hour or up to 24 hours in the fridge.

2 Heat a non-stick wok then add half the oil and stir-fry the carrots for 1 minute. Add the mushrooms and sugarsnap peas and cook for a further 1 minute over a high heat. Pour in 4 tablespoons water, cover the wok and cook for 1 minute more. Transfer to a bowl and set aside.

3 Wipe out the wok with kitchen paper, then add the remaining oil, over high heat. Add the ginger and remaining spring onions. Cook for about 30 seconds, stirring continuously, then add the liver and its marinade and cook for 1 minute, stirring all the time.

4 Add a splash of water to the liver to moisten, then return the vegetables to the wok and stir-fry for 1–2 minutes until all the ingredients are very hot.

5 Serve at once in warm bowls with the rice, garnished with coriander leaves.

PER SERVING: 308 kcals; 11g fat; 2g saturated fat; 31g carbohydrate; 0.45g sodium

Asian meatballs
with raw tomato sauce

A pleasant alternative to the classic Italian meatball dish, fresher, lighter, and containing all those Asian flavours. You can freeze the meatballs if you want.

SERVES 4

- **500g lean pork mince**
- **1 spring onion, finely chopped**
- **1 garlic clove, finely chopped**
- **3cm piece of fresh ginger, peeled and grated**
- **finely grated zest of 1 lime**
- **2 tablespoons chopped coriander**
- **1 tablespoon fish sauce (nam pla)**
- **1 small dessert apple, cored, grated and excess juice squeezed out**
- **1 tablespoon sweet chilli sauce**
- **1 tablespoon chopped cashew nuts**
- **250g rice or buckwheat noodles or quinoa spaghetti (pictured)**
- **shredded spring onion, to garnish**

FOR THE RAW TOMATO SAUCE

- **3 plum tomatoes, diced**
- **1 red chilli, de-seeded and finely chopped**
- **1 small red onion, finely chopped**
- **juice of 1 lime**
- **3 tablespoons chopped coriander**
- **1 tablespoon rapeseed oil**

1 Preheat the oven to 200ºC/400ºF/gas mark 6. For the meatballs, combine all the ingredients except the noodles and spring onion in a mixing bowl. With wetted hands, shape the mixture into small balls. Place in a roasting tin lined with baking parchment and cook in the oven for about 15 minutes, turning over once or twice, until opaque and cooked through.

2 Meanwhile, cook the noodles or pasta according to the manufacturer's instructions. Combine all the ingredients for the raw tomato sauce. Mix the two together and allow the pasta to warm the sauce.

3 Divide the pasta between four warm bowls and top with the meatballs and shredded spring onions.

PER SERVING: 449 kcals; 11g fat; 3g saturated fat; 57g carbohydrate; 0.48g sodium

desserts

Yes, you can have your cake and eat it. These desserts are only about 100 calories or less, and will finish off any meal. They are based on fruit, so you will also be getting one of your five-a-day – another great reason to try these recipes. Choose the berry desserts in summer and the pumpkin recipe later in the year, while the bacoffee pots are sophisticated enough for any dinner party.

souffléed pumpkin pie custards

This recipe takes its inspiration from the great American tradition of making pumpkin pie. Not only does it taste good, but it is another way to get some vegetables into your daily diet.

MAKES 6

- 1 x 425g tin solid pack pumpkin
- finely grated zest and juice of 1 orange
- 1 teaspoon ground cinnamon
- ½ teaspoon ground ginger
- pinch of ground cloves
- 2 tablespoons maple syrup
- 150ml semi-skimmed milk
- 1 egg, separated
- 1 teaspoon icing sugar, to dust

1 Preheat the oven to 180ºC/350ºF/gas mark 4.
2 Beat together all the ingredients except the egg white until smooth. Whisk the egg white until stiff then fold through the mixture. Divide between six 175ml ramekins.
3 Set the ramekins in a roasting tin and pour enough boiling water into the tin to come at least halfway up the sides of the ramekins.
4 Bake for 20-25 minutes until lightly set and warmed through. Serve warm, sprinkled with icing sugar.

PER SERVING: 77 kcals; 2g fat; 0.6g saturated fat; 12g carbohydrate; 0.08g sodium

summer berry fruits

Top these with a small dollop of natural yogurt or fromage frais and a bunch of redcurrants or a tiny sprig of mint, lemon balm or sweet cicely.

SERVES 4

- about 4 sheets gelatine (or enough to set 600ml)
- 400ml light cranberry juice
- 100ml diet American ginger ale
- 300g assorted berries: choose from small strawberries, raspberries, blackberries, blueberries
- 4 tablespoons fromage frais or natural yogurt (optional)
- 4 sprigs of mint, lemon balm or sweet cicely (optional)

1 Soak the gelatine sheets in cold water according to the instructions on the packet.
2 Warm half the cranberry juice in a small saucepan. Squeeze the excess water from the gelatine and stir into the warmed liquid until dissolved. Stir in the remaining juice and the ginger ale.
3 Halve or quarter the strawberries as necessary then arrange half the berries in four small glasses and pour over half the jelly. Chill until set then add the remaining berries and pour over the remaining liquid jelly. (Note: If you put all the fruit and jelly in at once the fruit will float to the top rather than be interspersed through the jelly.)
4 Chill until set. To serve, decorate with the fromage frais and herbs, if wished.

PER SERVING: 78 kcals; 1g fat; 0.7g saturated fat; 11g carbohydrate; 0.04g sodium

papaya and lime sorbet

The nicest texture is achieved with an ice-cream maker. If you haven't got one, freeze the mixture in a rigid plastic container then soften slightly and beat with a hand-held electric whisk or pulse in a food-processor until smooth. Freeze until required.

SERVES 4
- **2 papayas**
- **juice of 1 lime**
- **100ml diet tonic water**
- **½ teaspoon angostura bitters (optional)**

1 Halve the papayas and remove the seeds. Peel the fruit, roughly chop them and place in a liquidiser goblet or food-processor along with the lime juice. Purée until smooth.
2 Stir in the tonic water and bitters, if using, and transfer to an ice-cream maker. Churn until frozen. Serve at once or freeze until required.

PER SERVING: 49 kcals; 0.2g fat; 0g saturated fat; 12g carbohydrate; 0.01g sodium

Anna's iced berry crush

Almost like an instant cheesecake ice. Keep one of the shop-bought packs of fruit in your freezer and you can have this simple yet delicious dessert ready in 5 minutes!

SERVES 4
- **190g frozen summer berry selection**
- **250g tub quark**
- **2 tablespoons maple syrup**

1 Roughly crush the frozen berries in a food-processor, or in a bowl.
2 Stir together the quark and maple syrup and fold the berries through just so they give a ripple effect. Serve at once.

PER SERVING: 80 kcals; 0.1g fat; 0g saturated fat; 11g carbohydrate; 0.03g sodium

 **FOR WEIGHT MAINTENANCE** # Afghan milk jellies

A delicate and refreshing dessert for hot weather. Agar is a setting agent that does not require cold to set it – however these desserts should be kept in the fridge covered until you need them. Agar is suitable for vegetarians.

SERVES 4
- **500ml semi-skimmed milk**
- **8 green cardamom pods, bruised**
- **1 tablespoon golden caster sugar**
- **1 tablespoon agar flakes**
- **100g small green grapes, to decorate**

1 Pour the milk into a small saucepan and add the cardamom pods. Heat gently just until bubbles form on the surface of the milk where it touches the pan. Cover and leave for 1 hour until cooled.
2 Stir in the sugar then sprinkle the surface of the milk with the agar flakes. Warm gently without stirring then once warm, stir and simmer very gently for 3–5 minutes until the agar dissolves.
3 Strain to remove the cardamom then divide between four small glasses. Leave until set then cover and chill until required.
4 Halve or quarter the grapes and spoon them on top of the jellies.

PER SERVING: 83 kcals; 2g fat; 1g saturated fat; 12g carbohydrate; 0.06g sodium

seared pineapple
with pomegranate salsa

Searing slices of pineapple on a ridged grill pan allows the natural sugars on the surface to caramelise - delicious.

SERVES 4

- 1 medium-sized pineapple
- 25g pomegranate seeds (or redcurrants or strawberries, chopped)
- 1 tablespoon clear honey
- 2 teaspoons chopped mint
- ½ long red chilli, de-seeded (optional)

1 'Top and tail' the pineapple then using a sharp, serrated knife, cut away all the skin, removing the 'eyes' - the black indentations - as you go.
2 Cut the pineapple into 10 even slices. Reserve the 8 best slices for grilling. Discard the core from the remaining 2 slices and chop the flesh finely. Mix with the pomegranate seeds, honey and mint and set aside.
3 Set a non-stick ridged grill pan or non-stick frying pan over a high heat. Sear the chilli half just to soften it slightly then finely chop. Add 1 teaspoon to the salsa (more if you prefer).
4 Sear the reserved slices of pineapple for about 1 minute each side until lightly golden. You will need to do this in batches.
5 Serve at once with the salsa.

PER SERVING: 76 kcals; 0.3g fat; 0g saturated fat; 19g carbohydrate; 0g sodium

FOR WEIGHT MAINTENANCE

pears in nightshirts

Yes, you can eat pastry! The pears will soften and sweeten in the oven and will provide a contrasting texture to the crisp pastry.

SERVES 4

- 4 medium-ripe pears with stalks
- 25g stem ginger (2 small pieces), chopped
- 2 tablespoons quark
- 4 sheets filo pastry
- ½ teaspoon icing sugar

1 Preheat the oven to 200ºC/400ºF/gas mark 6.
2 Peel and core the pears from the base, ensuring the stalks remain intact.
3 Mix together the ginger and quark and use to stuff each pear.
4 Brush one sheet of filo with a little water then encase a pear. Set on a non-stick baking tray. Repeat with the remaining filo and 3 pears.
5 Bake for 35-40 minutes until crisp and golden. You may need to turn them during cooking so that they bake evenly.
6 Put the icing sugar in a fine sieve and sprinkle over the top of the pears. Serve at once.

PER SERVING: 111 kcals; 1g fat; 0.1g saturated fat; 25g carbohydrate; 0.14g sodium

strawberry tart

Cook the pastry up to 4 hours before required, but add the topping just before serving.

SERVES 6

- 4 sheets filo pastry
- 2 teaspoons unsalted butter, melted
- 1 tablespoon icing sugar
- 6 tablespoons fat-free fromage frais
- 1 tablespoon lemon curd
- 350g small strawberries, hulled and halved

1 Preheat the oven to 200°C/400°F/gas mark 6. Set a sheet of filo on a non-stick baking tray. Brush with a little melted butter and sprinkle with a little icing sugar. Repeat the layers three more times, reserving about 1 teaspoon of the icing sugar.

2 Bake the pastry for 10 minutes until golden. Leave to go cold.

3 Mix the fromage frais with the lemon curd and spread over the pastry. Top with the strawberries and sprinkle with the reserved icing sugar. Serve at once.

PER SERVING: 89 kcals; 2g fat; 1g saturated fat; 16g carbohydrate; 0.13g sodium

fresh figs
with rosewater foam gratin

Foam is very popular with chefs at the moment – this is my version to try at home. Rosewater is available in the baking section of supermarkets. Try using 250g strawberries and 150g blueberries instead of the figs and raspberries as a variation.

SERVES 4

- 2 medium eggs
- 2 tablespoons golden caster sugar
- 2 tablespoons rosewater
- 4 fresh figs
- 100g fresh raspberries

1 Choose a large glass bowl that fits over a saucepan. Half fill the saucepan with water and bring to a simmer.

2 Put the eggs and sugar in the bowl and set over the simmering water. Using a hand-held electric whisk, whisk the eggs and sugar to a thick foam that holds the trail of the whisk. Whisk in the rosewater a little at a time. Switch off the heat under the saucepan.

3 Preheat the grill to high. Cut the figs into six wedges each and arrange in four individual gratin dishes or saucers, with the raspberries. Spoon over the rosewater foam.

4 Set them under the grill for about 1 minute until lightly golden. Serve at once.

PER SERVING: 98 kcals; 3g fat; 0.8g saturated fat; 14g carbohydrate; 0.04g sodium

PER SERVING (WITH STRAWBERRIES AND BLUEBERRIES): 95 kcals; 3g fat; 0.8g saturated fat; 14g carbohydrate; 0.04g sodium

apple galette

A galette is a French crêpe or flatcake that can be made with puff pastry, pancake batter or a bread-like dough. I've used filo pastry and a classic French topping.

SERVES 2

- **2 teaspoons raisins**
- **2 sheets filo pastry**
- **1 teaspoon unsalted butter, melted**
- **1 dessert apple, cored, quartered and very thinly sliced then tossed with 1 teaspoon lemon juice**
- **1 teaspoon pine nuts, toasted**
- **½ teaspoon finely chopped fresh rosemary**
- **½ teaspoon icing sugar**

1 Preheat the oven to 220ºC/425ºF/gas mark 7. Just cover the raisins with boiling water and set aside.

2 Brush each sheet of filo with water and fold in half. Set one on a non-stick baking tray, brush with water and top with the second one. Bake for 10 minutes until lightly golden.

3 Brush the surface with melted butter. Casually arrange the apple slices to cover the surface of the pastry then sprinkle with the pine nuts and rosemary. Put the icing sugar in a small sieve and dust over the apples.

4 Bake the galette for 10 minutes until the apple is softened and the edges of the pastry are crispy and golden. Drain the raisins and sprinkle over. Serve at once.

PER SERVING: 118 kcals; 4g fat; 2g saturated fat; 20g carbohydrate; 0.14g sodium

roasted peaches with blueberries

SERVES 4

- **3-4 (about 500g) peaches**
- **1 vanilla pod, split lengthways**
- **large pinch of saffron strands**
- **150ml white grape juice**
- **100g blueberries**
- **25g barley flakes**
- **1 tablespoon unrefined demerara sugar**

1 Preheat the oven to 190°C/375°F/gas mark 5.

2 Quarter and stone the peaches and set them in a single layer in a baking dish. Add the vanilla pod, saffron and grape juice and bake, uncovered, for 20-30 minutes until tender. Switch off the oven.

3 Add the blueberries to the peaches and return to the oven to keep warm in the residual heat.

4 Meanwhile, toast the barley flakes in a non-stick frying pan over medium heat until lightly golden. Sprinkle in the sugar and allow to melt. Stir well and leave to go cold. Sprinkle over the peaches and serve at once.

PER SERVING: 99 kcals; 0.3g fat; 0g saturated fat; 24g carbohydrate; 0.01g sodium

stove-top plums
A quick and easy dessert.

SERVES 4

- **1 tablespoon unsalted butter**
- **1 tablespoon light muscovado sugar**
- **8 large red plums**

1 Put the butter and sugar in a large non-stick frying pan over medium heat until melted.

2 Stone and halve the plums and add to the pan. Cover and simmer for 10-15 minutes until tender.

PER SERVING: 100 kcals; 3g fat; 2g saturated fat; 18g carbohydrate; 0g sodium

basmati rice pudding with apricots

FOR WEIGHT MAINTENANCE

A light rice pudding – basmati rice has a lower GI than normal pudding rice.

SERVES 4

- **50g brown basmati rice**
- **300ml semi-skimmed milk**
- **1 tablespoon golden caster sugar**
- **4 apricots, halved and stoned**
- **1 fruit-flavoured tea bag of your choice**

1 Rinse the rice in a sieve under cold running water then transfer to a saucepan and cover with 300ml cold water. Leave to soak for 30 minutes.
2 Bring to a simmer then cover and simmer for 10-15 minutes until the rice is almost tender.
3 Add the milk and sugar and bring to a simmer. Simmer, covered, for 20-30 minutes, stirring occasionally until the rice is tender and the pudding has the consistency you prefer.
4 Meanwhile, put the apricot halves in a saucepan with the tea bag and 150ml cold water. Bring to a simmer then simmer, covered, for 5-10 minutes until tender. Remove from the heat and discard the tea bag.
5 Serve the apricots with the rice pudding.

PER SERVING: 103 kcals; 2g fat; 0.8g saturated fat; 20g carbohydrate; 0.06g sodium

mango fool (left)

FOR WEIGHT MAINTENANCE

Another very simple dessert recipe – it will make the perfect ending to a rich meal.

SERVES 4

- **1 large mango**
- **200g 8% fat fromage frais**

1 Cut the two 'cheeks' from the mango and set aside.
2 Cut all the rest of the flesh from around the stone, discarding any skin. Purée in a liquidiser goblet, adding a little of the fromage frais, if necessary, then stir in the rest of the fromage frais.
3 Peel and dice the reserved mango 'cheeks' and layer up in four glasses with the puréed mixture. Serve at once or cover and chill until required.

PER SERVING: 100 kcals; 4g fat; 2g saturated fat; 13g carbohydrate; 0.02g sodium

bacoffee pots (right)

FOR WEIGHT MAINTENANCE

Little pots but lots of flavour!

SERVES 4

- **2 teaspoons instant espresso coffee**
- **1 tablespoon dark muscovado sugar**
- **1 large banana, mashed**
- **250g fat-free fromage frais**
- **10g dark chocolate (72% cocoa solids), grated**
- **2 teaspoons flaked almonds, toasted**

1 Mix the coffee and sugar with 1 tablespoon boiling water to dissolve. Allow to cool then stir in the mashed banana and then fold in the fromage frais, keeping a slight ripple effect.
2 Transfer to four small glasses and chill until required. Top with chocolate and almonds before serving.

PER SERVING: 100 kcals; 2g fat; 0.7g saturated fat; 16g carbohydrate; 0.02g sodium

Index

Index

CONVERSION CHART

WEIGHT (solids)		VOLUME (liquids)	
7g	¼oz	5ml	1 teaspoon
10g	½oz	10ml	1 dessertspoon
20g	¾oz	15ml	1 tblsp or ½fl oz
25g	1oz	30ml	1fl oz
40g	1½oz	40ml	1½fl oz
50g	2oz	50ml	2fl oz
60g	2½oz	60ml	2½fl oz
75g	3oz	75ml	3fl oz
100g	3½oz	100ml	3½fl oz
110g	4oz (¼lb)	125ml	4fl oz
125g	4½oz	150ml	5fl oz (¼ pint)
150g	5½oz	160ml	5½fl oz
175g	6oz	175ml	6fl oz
200g	7oz	200ml	7fl oz
225g	8oz (½lb)	225ml	8fl oz
250g	9oz	250ml (0.25 litre)	9fl oz
275g	10oz	300ml	10fl oz (½ pint)
300g	10½oz	325ml	11fl oz
310g	11oz	350ml	12fl oz
325g	11½oz	370ml	13fl oz
350g	12oz (¾lb)	400ml	14fl oz
375g	13oz	425ml	15fl oz (¾ pint)
400g	14oz	450ml	16fl oz
425g	15oz	500ml (0.5 litre)	18fl oz
450g	1lb	550ml	19fl oz
500g (½kg)	18oz	600ml	20fl oz (1 pint)
600g	1¼lb	700ml	1¼ pints
700g	1½lb	850ml	1½ pints
750g	1lb 10oz	1 litre	1¾ pints
900g	2lb	1.2 litres	2 pints
1kg	2¼lb	1.5 litres	2½ pints
1.1kg	2½lb	1.8 litres	3 pints
1.2kg	2¾lb	2 litres	3½ pints
1.3kg	3lb		
1.5kg	3lb 5oz	**LENGTH**	
1.6kg	3½lb	5mm	¼ inch
1.8kg	4lb	1cm	½ inch
2kg	4½lb	2cm	¾in
2.25kg	5lb	2.5cm	1 inch
2.5kg	5½lb	3cm	1¼in
3kg	6½lb	4cm	1½in
		5cm	2 inches
		7.5 cm	3 inches
		10cm	4 inches
		15cm	6 inches
		18cm	7 inches
		20cm	8 inches
		24cm	10 inches
		28cm	11 inches
		30 cm	12 inches